ENDORSEMENTS

Based on historical analysis, Samuel Lee demonstrates how women have been treated and played an active role in each era of Japanese history. *Japanese Women & Christianity* is an important book that informs about women's achievements in numerous domains such as politics, welfare, culture, pop culture, and education, and how women contributed to the formation and growth of society in each century. My appreciation to the author for his warm and affirming attitude toward women, as well as for his high regard for women and belief in their potential. *Japanese Women & Christianity* allows Japan to reflect on the past and re-examine the role that women play in society and in the world.

Dr. Eiko Takamizawa
Editorial board for the *Journal of the Japan Missiological Society*
Former professor of Intercultural Studies at Torch Trinity Graduate University
Seoul, South Korea

In *Japanese Women & Christianity*, Samuel Lee emphasizes the tremendous contribution that Japanese women of faith have made by drawing on church history, personal tales, gender studies, and cultural analysis. Lee illustrates the unique contributions that context has on a greater understanding of faith and culture by delving deeply into the particularities of Japanese women and Christianity. He brings to light an often overlooked narrative: the story of Japanese women and Christianity. Samuel Lee's important work brings to light an invisible story–that of Japanese women and Christianity.

Nikki Toyama-Szeto,
Executive Director, Christians for Social Action
Co-editor, More than Serving Tea (IVP)

ENDORSEMENTS

Samuel Lee provides this invaluable collection of Christian Japanese women's biographical sketches, deftly interwoven with concise historical analysis. Highlighting Christian women in Japan is a long overdue and desperately needed contribution, particularly for an English-language audience. While drawing on other biographers' labors, Lee has creatively compiled an original study that will no doubt open many doors for further study of Japan's many heroines of the Christian movement.

Rev. Dr. J. Nelson Jennings
Editor, *Global Missiology - English*
Author of *Theology in Japan: Takakura Tokutaro (1885-1934)* and
God the Real Superpower: Rethinking our Role in Missions

Christian women in Japan are being rooted in the source of wisdom and truth. They have spoken out and acted on basic issues so often overlooked by others. They have been on the cutting edge, ahead of their time, and have therefore led the way for many women.

Mine Watanabe

Japanese
WOMEN
& CHRISTIANITY

ISBN: 978-90-79516-04-9

Academy Press of Amsterdam
P.O. Box 12429 • 1100 AK Amsterdam
The Netherlands
apa.eu.com

Layout & Design
timmyroland.com

CONTENTS

A Note on Japanese Names

The Japanese custom of listing names begins with the surname; however, I used the English approach, which places the surname last. Except in a few cases, names in this book are accompanied by birth and death dates, when available.

PREFACE

My interest in Japan dates back to my childhood when I was only eight or nine years old. Watching Japanese anime and samurai films at the time piqued my curiosity about the culture and history of the Japanese people. After high school, I decided to study cultural anthropology and development sociology in the Faculty of Social Sciences at Leiden University, with Japan positioned as my regional specialty. During my years there, one of the elective courses that I took was Feminism, despite being the only man in the class. Our evaluation that term took the shape of a writing project, and I chose to write about women's rights and feminism in Japan, which resulted in a project exceeding 30 pages. During that time, back in the early 1990s, I thus became keenly interested in the roles of women in Japanese culture and society.

Many years later, in the early 2000s, as a Christian, I also became interested not only in the relationship between Christianity and Japan but also why, despite centuries of missionary work, Christianity has always been a minority religion in Japan. Those fields of study encouraged me to pursue a doctorate in the Faculty of Theology at Vrije Universiteit Amsterdam. As a result, the topic of women in Japan became rekindled through my studies but from a Christian viewpoint. Although I had considered publishing a book on women's roles in Christianity in Japan, it was not until I read Haruko Nawata Ward's *Women Religious Leaders in Japan's Christian Century, 1549–1650,* that I began writing about Christianity and women in Japan. I want to convey my heartfelt appreciation to Dr. Ward for allowing me to quote from her work. My thanks also go to all of the writers whose works are cited in my book, all of whom have been a ceaseless source of inspiration for me.

I hope that this book serves as a statement of solidarity with all women in the world and as a call for awakening my fellow men to fight against the unjust patriarchal systems that dominate the Christian church and society at large.

Japanese WOMEN & CHRISTIANITY

SAMUEL LEE

Academy Press of Amsterdam

INTRODUCTION

When traveling across Japan, residents and tourists alike may sometimes encounter signboards stating *Nyonin Kinsei* what translates from Japanese into "No Women Permitted." Although *Nyonin Kinsei* was abolished during the Meiji Restoration in 1872, the tradition persists today (Takemaru 2010, 14).

In contemporary Japan, despite being a nation home to cutting-edge technology, centuries-old traditions, customs, and religious beliefs restrict women from, for example, visiting certain holy sites and regions during tunnel building, when women's presence is believed to enrage the mountain deity. Women are also prohibited from climbing specific sections of sacred mountains—for instance, past a particular point on Mount Omine. World-famous sumo wrestling matches have also caused controversy, for women are not allowed to step into the wrestling ring due to a belief that their presence will defile the space. In fact, when two prominent women officials, Mayumi Moriyama, Japan's chief cabinet secretary, and Fusae Ōta, Osaka's governor, tried to enter sumo rings in 1990 and 2000, respectively, they were denied by the Japan Sumo Association. Women also remain prohibited from participating in *kabuki*, a 400-year-old Japanese style of theater and dance that began with all-women casts but was banned in 1629 due to its potential to corrupt public morals. Since then, *kabuki* has been performed exclusively by men (Takemaru 2010, 15).

Women activists who organize against the custom of excluding women are usually regarded as problematic. According to traditionalists and nationalists, some of whom are themselves women, such customs should be maintained in their current form to preserve centuries-old religious and cultural traditions for future generations. Thus, Akiko Yosano's (1878–1942) poem, "The Day the Mountains Move," presented in Chapter 2, has yet to be wholly realized owing to the persistent tradition of excluding women, even in 21st-century Japan.

Throughout its early periods, Japan was a matriarchal society. Indeed, Japan's history, at least from a mythological standpoint, begins with a woman: Amaterasu Omikami, the sun goddess, from whom all beings derive. Beyond that, both the *Kojiki* and *Nihonshoki*, two ancient Japanese written records, depict women as the essence of excellence and the embodiment of purity, intelligence, and beauty through the personification of Amaterasu Omikami. Women are also sovereigns, shamans, and chieftains in Japanese mythology and, believed to be more divine than men and performed sacred ceremonies (Takemaru 2010, 9).

The History of the Kingdom of Wei (297 CE), an ancient Chinese record on Japan, mentions that a shaman priestess ruled over the land of Wa, now modern-day Japan. The priestess is thought to be Himiko (170–248 CE), also known as Pimiko, who is recognized as being the sovereign of Japan in the 3rd century CE (Takemaru 2010, 9). Even though stories about the goddess Amaterasu Omikami can be found in the *Kojiki* and *Nihonshoki*, none of them mention the existence of Himiko, which has led Barbra Ambros (2015, 11) to characterize Himiko as an enigmatic figure and to debate her existence. Ambros (2015, 12) notes that Himiko's identity has been a source of contention among historians, some of whom understand "Himiko" to be a title, not a given name, thereby implying that Himiko may relate to the religious role of *Miko* ('shaman'), not the governing role of empress. Regardless of Himiko's role, between 593 and 770 CE, Japan did have six empresses, including two who reigned twice, for a total of eight imperial reigns by women. Empress Suiko (554–628) reigned from 592 to 628 CE before the Nara period (710–794), Empress Kōgyoku (594–661), who reigned twice, Empress Jitō (645–703), Empress Meisho (1624–1696) from 1629 to 1643, and, most recently, Go-Sakuramachi (1740–1813) from 1762 to 1813.

Before the early Heian period (794–1185), Japanese society was matriarchal, with descendants along matrilineal lines inheriting property. During the Asuka period (538–710), women played an essential role in the transformations shaping Japan as a new nation. To this day, the impact of those heroines echoes throughout the Asuka area.[1] The introduction of Buddhism into Japan in 552 CE sparked religious and political upheaval as conflicts arose between proponents of preserving Shinto as Japan's religion and people who embraced Buddhism. Empress Suiko, the first empress in Japan, succeeded in making peace between Buddhist and Shinto adherents and thus cultivated a balanced fusion between Shinto and Buddhism in Japan. As a Shinto priestess, she promoted Japan's traditional Shinto values while endorsing the newly introduced religion during the Asuka and early Nara periods, when the persecution of Buddhists threatened social harmony. It is also believed that Japan's first Buddhist nun was Chujo Hime (753–781), who

---

1 http://asuka-japan-heritage.jp/global/en/about/

later took the name Zenshin-ni and has since become a folk heroine in Japanese history. A daughter in the family of the court noble Fujiwara of Toyonari, she escaped the cruelties of her stepmother by fleeing to the kingdom of Baekje in Korea, where she studied Buddhist precepts. Upon returning to Japan, she dedicated her life to spreading Buddhism and guiding believers into the priesthood and, in time, became a nun at Taima-dera in Nara.

During the Taika Reforms in 645, Kōgyoku ascended the imperial throne twice—first as Empress Kōgyoku and later as Empress Saimei—and, in her role, became renowned for her leadership and large-scale civil engineering projects, including the construction of imperial palaces. Likewise, Empress Jitō, another woman leader in the Asuka period, supervised the completion of the new Capital of Fujiwara-Kyo, which encompassed the three mountains of Yamato.

She also ensured the establishment of the Taihō Code, which marked the founding of Japan as a nation with a full-fledged central government.[2] Beyond governance and construction, literature was also enriched by the contributions of women during the Asuka period. Japan's oldest compilation of poetry, *Man'yoshu (Collection of Ten-Thousand Leaves)*, is believed to have been coauthored by Empress Jito and Lady Nukata.

During the Nara period (710–794), Buddhism, as a relatively new religion in Japan, continued to negotiate its place in the nation's politics, culture, and society. According to Ambros (2015, 55), Buddhism welcomed women throughout the Nara period, and women monastics, just as their male counterparts, formed part of the state-sponsored temple

---

2 http://asuka-japan-heritage.jp/global/en/about/

system and performed priestly duties just as men did. However, such inclusion gradually waned, especially after the second reign of Empress Kōken, then known as Empress Shōtoku (764–770). A follower of Buddhism, Empress Shōtoku facilitated the religion's influence in Japanese politics. In 764, she appointed priest Dōkyō (700–772) as a grand minister, who was promoted as priestly emperor two years later (Ambros 2015, 50). However, her partiality toward Buddhism was not tolerated by Japanese society, nor was her commissioned printing of a million prayer charms. Thus, in the years after her rule, women became excluded not only from Buddhist monastic society but also from the imperial succession.

After Empress Shōtoku died in 770, the status of women in the imperial court weakened considerably, and no women sovereigns ruled again until the Tokugawa period (1603–1868). Along with their reduced political role, women's governmental responsibilities as officials in the public domain continued to decline as well. As a case in point, Princess Inoue, the principal consort who once stood alongside Emperor Kōnin (708–782) as a ruler and had the right to succession after her husband's death, now stood below her spouse. In time, most imperial consorts and their relatives served at court, which served to emphasize, if not increase, the participation of noblewomen in the private sphere (Adolphson, Kamens and Matsumoto 2007, 19).

In 784, the imperial capital was moved to Nagaoka-Kyo and, in 794, at the beginning of the Heian period, relocated to Heian-Kyo (present day Kyoto). The Heian period is considered to be the golden age of Japanese aristocratic culture. It was expected from the upper class, both men and women, to be educated in music, writing, and fashion. In turn, poetry became a highly esteemed art form, and quoting verse and demonstrating knowledge of poems were regarded as signs of prestige. Unlike men, however, women were not allowed to write using Chinese characters, for it was believed that Chinese was of higher status than Japanese and should be used exclusively by men, who outranked women in court culture and society in general. Thanks to that limitation, women in the imperial court, restricted to using Japanese only, adapted a writing system called *hiragana*, which men would later come to use as well. As *hiragana* became popular among commoners and increasingly used in poems and short stories, primarily written by women, Japanese poetry and literature written by women began to flourish.

In that way, Japan's lay literature and language have their roots in women's writing (Takemaru 2019, 10). Among the many women authors during the Heian period, ones from the imperial court included Ono no Komachi (708–782), Izumi Shikibu (dates unknown), Sei Shōnagon (966–1017 or 1025), and Shikibu Murasaki (973–1014 or 1025). Their works are widely read and studied to this day, including the legendary *Genji Monogatari (The Tale of Genji)* by Murasaki (Takemaru 2010, 10).

As members of the court, noblewomen played important roles at court and in palace affairs during the Heian period. They could also own property, receive education, and, if discrete, take lovers. However, those freedoms were mostly limited to women in court and not extended to women among the commoners. Even though aristocratic women were thus relatively privileged during the Heian period and enjoyed a certain degree of autonomy, they were excluded from public affairs. Ambros (2015, 51) has argued that doctrines of Buddhism that restrict women, including the Five Obstructions, the Three Obediences,[3] and the requirement of woman-to-man transformations to attain Buddhahood, became magnified during the Heian period. In parallel, both Buddhism and Shinto beliefs associating women with impurity and sinfulness became widespread (Takemaru 2010, 10). In particular, women were considered to be instruments of evil who would tempt and seduce men away from salvation—that is, the achievement of Buddhahood. Buddhism at the time thus imposed strict physical limitations upon women and did not permit them to be seen by men and sometimes even other women (Silva 2010). Because Heian Buddhism generally considered men to be the personification of Buddha and women to be evil, women gradually became relegated to a submissive role in Japanese society.[4]

During the medieval period in Japan (1185–1600), women functioned only to serve their fathers, husbands, and sons throughout their lives.[5] Women at the time observed a well-known manta, one even occasionally used today, namely, "As a young girl, a woman obeys her father; upon marriage,

---

3 "Five barriers and three obediences" refers to the obstacles that hinder women from achieving Buddhahood. The "three obediences," also known as the "three submissions," were a Brahmanic and Confucian rule of behavior that required women to obey their parents as children, their husbands after marriage, and their sons in old age.

4 "Women in Buddhism." https://stellarhousepublishing.com/women-in-buddhism/

5 Japan's medieval history is classified into three significant periods: the Kawamura period (1185–1333), the Muromachi period (1333–1568), and the Azuchi period (1568–1600).

she obeys her husband; and when widowed, she must then obey her son."[6] Thus, as soon as a woman married, she was expected to bear her husband a son, and unlike widowed men, widowed women could never remarry. With those roles in place, Japanese culture evolved into a patrilineal society in the 14th century, when wives moved into their husbands' households.

In medieval Japan, women were classified into four strata: commoners, geishas, aristocrats, and, albeit not as well-known, samurais. Counter to the stereotype of the man-oriented world of samurais, women during the medieval period could train as samurais and be expected to use their samurai skills during war and emergencies to protect their homes and families while their husbands were on the battlefield.[7] Even so, samurai women were expected to submit to the men in their families.

Women warriors continued to exist until the end of the Tokugawa period, as exemplified by Yae Neesima (1845–1932).[8] A warrior before becoming a Christian and marrying her husband Joseph (Jo), Neesima aided in the defense of Tsuruga Castle when, in October 1868, troops of the new Meiji government entered the Aizu region and laid siege to the structure. During the month-long Battle of Aizu, the castle was defended well, partly by Neesima, who, as a young woman, disguised herself as a samurai, seized leadership of

---

6 "Medieval Japan: Women's Role in Society." https://medievjapan. weebly.com/role-of-women-in-society.html

7 "Medieval Japan: Women's Role in Society." https://medievjapan. weebly.com/role-of-women-in-society.html

8 Yae Neesima was the wife of Joseph (Jo) H. Neesima (1843–1890), a well-known Christian in Japan.

a rifle unit in the castle, and fought alongside men to protect the town's residents (Yamashita 2009, 4).

In the eras that followed medieval Japan, which saw Francis Xavier's (1506–1552) arrival in 1549, the restriction of Christianity and the persecution of Christians from the mid-16th to the late 19th centuries, and Christianity's reentry into Japan in 1868 during the nation's modernization, Christianity dramatically altered women's roles and influence in Japanese religious culture and society. Even so, similar to other Japanese faiths, Christianity, as a Eurocentric patriarchal system, continues to restrict women's roles in the church in contemporary Japan.

Against that background, this book describes the significant roles that women in Japan have played since the arrival of Christianity. Women in Japan have contributed to Christianity's growth in the nation for nearly five centuries, especially by promoting theological discussions and engaging in political, social, and cultural activism. They have also contributed to charitable work, human rights, the fine arts, literature, and music. When Christianity was outlawed in Japan and Christians were persecuted (ca. 1565–1873), women even chose martyrdom and died for their faith in Jesus Christ.

Of course, similar to many other Christian women worldwide, Christian women in Japan have accomplished far more than what this book details. That being said, the book represents a work composed in solidarity by a brother, friend, and fellow scholar who chooses to stand alongside women and ensure that their stories are heard by women and men alike and never forgotten. Men in particular need to learn about the experiences of women from around the world, including Christian women of Japan, the subject of this book. The narrative presented herein, structured in a historically chronological way, is the product of a thorough examination of scholarly works published in English by famous historians, theologians, and sociologists, both Japanese and non-Japanese, and primarily by women— among others, Haruko Nawata Ward, Hisako Kinukawa, Tomoko Yamashita, Barbara Ambros, and Naoko Takemaru.

The book's narrative begins with the arrival of Christianity in Japan during the Tokugawa period and ends with contemporary Japan. Each chapter first offers an overview of the historical, political, and social events that transpired during the era that it covers. Each chapter also explores the overall status of women in Japanese society and culture in the era that it addresses, followed by a detailed description of the role of Christian women in Japan at the time. Each chapter discusses some, but not all, notable women in Christianity in Japan.

Chapter 1
Devoted to the Tokugawa period, recounts the emergence of Christianity in Japan and its significance. To illuminate the role of Christian women in Japan during the era, Haruko Nawata Ward's *Women Religious Leaders in Japan's Christian Century, 1549–1650* served as a primary English-language source. From the 16th to 19th centuries, women such as Julia Naitō (1566–1627) and Gracia Tama Hosokawa (aka Garasha in Japanese) (1563–1600) played various roles in Christianity in Japan—as translators, writers, teachers (e.g., catechists and apologists), debaters, lecturers, evangelists, charity workers, and champions of social causes—even in an era when women in Japan and worldwide had few rights.

Chapter 2

Continues with the Meiji period, during which Japan began its era of modernization, especially with the Meiji Restoration in 1868. During that period, not only did feminism arise in Japan, with Christianity serving to some degree as a source of inspiration, but the foundation for Christian women's education was established as well, and many Christian women in prewar and postwar Japan emerged as a result. Christian women thus gradually became involved in evangelism, social work, and advocacy for women's human rights and right to education. A prime example is Umeko Tsuda (1864–1929), who believed that all women in Japan should have equal access to higher education and that only education could help improve women's status in the country. Putting those ideas in practice, she established an institute for women to study English that after World War II became Tsuda University, one of the most prestigious women's colleges in Japan. In 1905, Tsuda also became the first president of the Japanese branch of the World Young Women's Christian Association.

Chapter 3

Describes an era that ushered in what is known as Taishō democracy, which lasted from 1912 to 1926 and was followed by the more limited, authoritarian regime of Emperor Hirohito's prewar Shōwa Empire. Women's education, which took root during the Meiji period, bore fruit in the form of notable women academics, activists, authors, and theologians, some of whose work continued into the late postwar era. Hatsune Hasegawa (1890–1979) and Tamaki Kawado Uemura (1890–1982) were among the first women pastors in Japan at the time, and Ginko Ogino (1851–1913) became the first woman doctor in Japan to receive a degree in Western medicine. Ogino married Yukiyoshi Shikata, a

Protestant minister, in 1890, and in 1894, she relocated with him to Hokkaido where they operated a medical practice. In 1908, following her husband's death, she returned to Tokyo and began running a hospital. She was also a member of the Woman's Christian Temperance Union.

Chapter 4

Examines the role of Christian women in Japan from 1945 to the present. War-torn Japan spurred women activists and groups, both Christian and non-Christian, to be increasingly engaged in lobbying, peacebuilding, and anti-nuclear action. After World War II, inspired by their faith, Christian women in Japan contributed to many art forms, including literature, cinema, manga (i.e., Japanese cartoons), and music. Among them, Machiko Hasegawa (1920–1992) was one of Japan's first women manga artists. Added to her, Kelly Kozumi Shinozawa, a contemporary Christian manga artist became known for her works *The Manga Messiah* and *The Manga Bible Series*, which have been translated into 21 languages worldwide. Japanese feminist theology additionally took shape during the period, led by notable women theologians, including Satoko Yamaguchi, a well-known feminist theologian who works both in Japan and worldwide; Haruko Nawata Ward, a historian known for her *Women Religious Leaders in Japan's Christian Century, 1549–1650*; and Rita Nakashima Brock (1950–), who in 1988 became the first Asian American woman to receive a doctorate in theology.

Chapter 5

Explores the role of women in modern Japanese society and culture and the challenges that they have faced. By doing so, I want to encourage Christians, including theologians, evangelists, activists, artists, and church leaders to address the pressing concerns confronting women in Japan in general. Historically, women have performed many of the day-to-day activities and social roles within the church. Although they represent the majority of churchgoers today, women remain in the minority when it comes to positions of decision-making in the church, including as heads of committees and boards. That trend reflects society at large in Japan, which ranked 120th out of 156 countries in the 2021 Gender Gap Report.[9]

Mine Watanabe rightfully suggests, "Christian women in Japan are being rooted in the source of wisdom and truth. They have spoken out and acted on basic issues so often overlooked by others. They have been on the cutting edge, ahead of their time, and have therefore led the way for many women" (Watanabe 1991, 131).

I end this introductory chapter with a poem that I once wrote inspired by the Japanese Christian poet Raichō Hiratsuka (1886–1971), who wrote, "In the beginning, the woman was truly the sun. An authentic person. Now she is the moon, a wan and sickly moon, dependent on another, reflecting another's brilliance":

Mother Church
In the beginning, the Church was a woman:
the bride of the morning star, a mother by nature.
Thus, she was called *Mother Church!*

She creates; she births sons and daughters.
Yet, for centuries, she has been silenced by her sons,
denied her existence, required to be silent and submissive.

---

9   Global Gender Gap Report 2021, World Economic Forum http://www.weforum.org/reports/global-gender-gap-report-2021

WOMEN & CHRISTIANITY

in the Tokugawa Period, 1603-1868

Chapter One

WOMEN & CHRISTIANITY
in the Tokugawa Period, 1603-1868

The early 17th century marked the beginning of a new chapter in Japanese history. In 1600, Ieyasu Tokugawa's victory in the Battle of Sekigahara allowed him to develop an army, which gradually led to the unification of Japan under the Tokugawa clan. As a result, the Tokugawas not only grew stronger militarily but also matured economically into a wealthy clan, and from 1603 to 1868, the Tokugawas ruled Japan.

Before the Tokugawa period, authority was exercised through paternalistic structures of social organization, with stratifications channeled from the top down according to personal ties. However, that form of stratification changed during the Tokugawa period. Japanese society began to differentiate into segments of varying hierarchical status, guided by each segment's systematic division into self-supporting units such as the military class *(kumi)*, the village *(mura)*, and the district *(machi)*. The position of the individual also changed during the period, when all individuals were regarded in the context of their social status based on their group or unit. Once determined, lines of status and group created vertical and horizontal boundaries within which the individual could move. Because society was divided according to levels of status and administrative units, personal power was limited, and control no longer rested in the hands of one person but an administrative system.

Decreasing personal power, along with the formation of legal units, prompted a desire for Confucianism as a solution to the problems in society. Based on the premise of natural separation between status and profession, Confucianism emphasizes loyalty and superior authority and, as such, was readily embraced by the Tokugawas as a means of governance. The idealistic aspect of Confucianism is that individuals should not seek to exceed their status, which was not always the case in practice. According to that doctrine, individuals' rights and obligations must not only function from the bottom to the top but also the other way around. For example, Confucianism established rules regarding rights and duties in Japanese society that differ by class and by status within and outside social classes. All of those rules take root in the family and prescribe the roles of the different members therein, with the father occupying the highest position. In that way, Confucianism established certain obligations and rules for all men and women that served to regulate people's behavior within society, from the family to the government. Thus, during the nearly three centuries of the Tokugawa period, people in Japan were forced to abide by rigid Confucian rules, and Confucianism functioned as the guideline for cultural, social, economic, and political life in the country.

The Tokugawa period is also regarded as including Japan's transition to modernization that would follow during the Meiji period. In "The Tokugawa Period and Japan's Preparation for Modern Economic Growth," Sydney Crawcour (1974) has posited that the roots of Japan's modernization should be sought in the Tokugawa period, especially in the rapid changes in the last 50 years of the period. Among them, traditional labor services were replaced by wage labor, subsistence farming gave way to commercial farming, and rural industry expanded. New commercial networks were also established through the official ratification of trade channels, and several Western-style industrial factories even emerged in the last years of the period (Crawcour 1974, 114).

However, in the final years of the Tokugawa period, as feudalism faded, social discontent grew, and the Shogun was consistently blamed for society's ills. The emperor, who had had little say during the period, increasingly attracted people's attention and was often hailed as the direct relative of the sun goddess. Shintoism also spread during the period's later years, and, with it, new nationalistic feelings. Due to the population's discontent and unrest in the land, the Shogun relinquished power in 1867. The Tokugawa period thus ended but not without leaving deep marks in Japanese society that remain to this day.

Women in the Tokugawa Period

As stated before, Confucian laws assign each individual to a particular social class based on their social and biological (i.e., sex and age) background, and women were no exception. Indeed, women's places in society differed starkly depending on their social status. However, despite ample literature about Tokugawa society, women are mentioned only rarely, usually concerning works written during the period.

One of the period's most famous instructional books, *Onna Daigaku (School of Women)*, from the early 18th century, describes the roles and duties of women in Confucian society. In particular, the text instructs parents to raise their daughters to be submissive in preparation to marry into other families, where exercising too much independence would be impertinent. As women, their most desirable qualities would be obedience, chastity, compassion, and emotional balance. Wives were expected to revere their husbands as if they were deities and to never become jealous or else they would risk alienating their husbands. If husbands misbehaved, wives were permitted to comment on their misconduct in a low voice only, and if the behavior persisted, wives could do nothing but wait for their husbands to repent. Later in this chapter, I discuss how such rules encouraged women to opt for a foreign faith newly introduced to Japan: Christianity or, more precisely, Roman Catholicism.

Although *Onna Daigaku* has sometimes been attributed to a Confucian scholar, Ekiken Kaibara (1630–1714), the author is his wife (Meyvis and Vande Walle 1989, 141). The work has also been characterized as a prescription for the samurai class, along with commoners and members of the agricultural class. Though the recurring theme of such writings was that women, especially in the samurai class, were subordinate to men, whether women abided by rules such as those in *Onna Daigaku* remains unclear. What is clear, however, is that the status of women, encompassing their labor activities and roles in the family and society, differed significantly depending on their social class and region, especially if they resided in parts of Japan where women acted as heads of their families.

Although anthropological works on women's status in Tokugawa society have proven valuable, they remain few and far between. Locating and accessing them, especially ones written in commonly used Western languages, are therefore laborious and usually lead researchers to a dead end. Of those works, one of the most important is Anne Walthall's (1991) "The Life Cycle of Farm Women in Tokugawa Japan" in the collection *Recreating Japanese Women, 1600–1945*, edited by Gail Lee Bernstein. This section of the chapter draws from Walthall's work, which itself is primarily based on various sources from the Tokugawa period, including village reports, population registries, petitions, passports, and hereditary reports. Other less-referenced sources are handbooks with guidelines for women's conduct and descriptions of her rights and obligations, which are less reliable, according to Walthall, because they do not purport real-life situations. Still, other sources, and arguably the most important, are family histories and diaries kept by wealthy farmer families in the 19th century. Notable examples of such texts include the Suzuki Bokushi family diaries from the Echigo region, the Sekiguchi family diaries from the village of Namamugi near Yokohama, and the family history of the Suzuki Heikuros from a village in Tama, a region near Tokyo.

Those sources suggest that parents made little distinction between children based on their sex when they were born, an event that could entail multiple ceremonies. According to Walthall (1991, 44), the choice of ceremony or ceremonies did not depend on the child's sex but on the family's economic well-being, the time of birth, and the stage of life of the other family members. The more or less equal treatment of children based on sex during the early years of the period troubled some Confucian scholars, who disagreed that daughters should receive as much attention as sons. As children grew, however, the concept of gender became increasingly critical, as shown by visible distinctions in certain rituals and rites of passage during their development. Gender-specific tasks were also made increasingly clear to children as they matured. Although the geographic location, economic conditions, and historical changes primarily determined what sort of woman

5

a girl would become in the Tokugawa period, all girls were expected to be polite, modest, obedient, and clean (Walthall 1991, 45).

In the Japanese language, the distinction between sex and gender would have also become apparent in the use of certain suffixes. In general, the suffix -sei has been used to indicate sex, such that josei is feminine and dansei masculine. Nowadays, however, only -danjo is used to indicate both sexes and genders. By contrast, gender would have been signified by -rashii, such that a female-like person, whether a man or woman, would be called onnarashii and a male-like person otokorashii (Robertson 1992, 167).

In nearly every village during the period, girls and boys were separated and engaged in different activities. Although some families in certain parts of Japan invested money in training their daughters in temples, girls were usually trained in needle shops (ohariya) and/or girls' rooms (musume yado), where they would learn how to take care of the household in anticipation of marrying into another family. In any case, before marriage, all girls were expected to have developed a strong command of household rules and tasks. Thus, during a typical day, girls would assist their mothers with the housework of their own families, and in the evening, they would attend a musume yado to learn all kinds of handicrafts, including sewing or weaving. Beyond such training, Dore (1965, 254) has estimated that 40% of Japanese boys in Tokugawa society but only 10% of girls were afforded an education. As that research also revealed, the 4-to-1 ratio could vary widely, however. The merchant class, for instance, was probably more willing to spend money on their daughters' education, for it was beneficial for a shop owner's wife or daughter(s) to be able to read and write and thus help to run the shop. Some farming families also pursued education for their daughters, albeit depending on the region and the family's economic status. In the early 19th century, wealthier farmers became increasingly aware of the advantage of having well-educated daughters who had learned more than what their mothers could teach them. Most likely, having a daughter receive an education was pursued as a mark of affluence to distinguish the family as being able to take better care of their children, including their daughters, who would reap the benefits of marrying into more affluent families as a result.

Getting married—on average, at the age of 14 to 15 years—brought about a metamorphosis in the life of a young woman and conferred a new status that she was expected to observe. Although some young women never married because they were required to help their parents until the end of their lives, most did. Leaving their native villages for the villages of their husbands, new brides confronted the disadvantages of entering into entirely new families and becoming subject to new family rules and traditions. Achieving harmony was a priority in the family and a task primarily charged to wives, one that they executed by not arguing or quarreling with the in-laws, performing the work expected of their position, and adjusting to all adversity (Walthall 1991, 55). If a new wife could not adapt to the new household or, according to the in-laws, was not sufficiently trained to perform her new duties, she was returned to her own family in disgrace.

The living circumstances of wives during the Tokugawa period varied depending on the family's class and economic situation. Wives in the samurai class lived under more stringent rules of Confucianism than their counterparts in the trading and farming classes. Because the samurai class was the most important in the period, samurai families acted as role models for families in other classes, who generally sought to emulate the samurai lifestyle—for example, in the education of their children—as a means to gain status. In general, however, wives were considered to be unclean, expected to be submissive to their husbands, and confined to doing housework and raising children. Wives rarely had the opportunity to become the heads of their households, and even if they did receive an education, it was only to further entrench their femininity and their observance of obligations that Confucianism demanded of them.

Regarding her status in the labor market, whether a woman could perform work depended heavily on the cultural and religious views of the period. In farming households, for instance, wives worked alongside their husbands in the field, often for economic reasons, or else did men's work in other households for only half a man's wages, although the rate would later rise to two-thirds of a man's wages. In any case, a potent combination of Shintoism, Buddhism, and popular belief validated the idea that women were naturally impure and should thus be barred from certain professions and even from entering certain workshops. A representative caution from the Tokugawa period reads, "When a woman enters a brewery, you will see that the *saké* [rice wine] becomes sour"!

As Japan's oldest industry, *saké*'s origins have been deliberated in light of three theories, all of which take women into account. First, according to the ancient historical chronicles the *Kojiki* and *Nihonshoki*, as Lebra (1991, 131–132) has posited, a goddess named Konohana Sukaya Hime chewed rice for so long that it began to ferment, hence the birth of *saké*. The second theory assumes that the virgin girls in ancient times chewed for so long that the enzymes in their mouths caused the rice to ferment, after which they spat the chewed rice into jars and sealed them for three days. The third theory comes from Okinawa, where girls approximately 14 years old are supposed to have sat in a circle around a big pot, chewed rice until their jaws hurt, and spit the chewed rice into the pot.

Interestingly, in Chinese, brewers are called *toji*, which in ancient times meant 'madam' or 'dame' and in contemporary Japan means 'brewmaster' (Lebra 1991, 131–132). The tragedy of the stories in all theories is that girls were thought to have originally developed and practiced the craft of *saké* brewing, whereas women in Tokugawa society were not even allowed to enter breweries. According to popular belief at the time, the spirit of the *saké* was feminine, and when a woman entered a brewery, she would arouse the jealousy of the *saké* spirit and spoil the *saké* being produced. Although rare, exceptions did occur that allowed women to brew *saké*, as in the Aizu Wakamatsu region, where women were thought to produce the best *saké* in the area. To become able to brew, women carried a token that rendered them clean and thus not subject to the jealousy of the saké spirit (Lebra 1991, 132).

The theories of *saké*'s origin and the exception of the Aizu Wakamatsu region suggest some remarkable sociological trends. Ancient myths and chronicles suggest that, in ancient times, women brewed *saké*, whereas that practice was next to impossible during the Tokugawa period due to various negative views about women. To place the change in attitude in its historical context, in Japan's distant past women's status differed starkly from their status in more recent centuries. In the former family system, based on so-called "visiting marriage," the marital residence and inheritance law were determined matrilineally. The new husband went to live with his bride's family or clan, where he was less able to impose his will (Meijvis and Vande Walle 1989, 132–133). However, the ever-increasing importance of military operations and the introduction of Confucianism and, to a lesser extent, Buddhism justified shifting the responsibility of the visiting marriage to women instead of men.

The interpretations and the creation of the popular views mentioned, including the jealousy of the *saké* spirit, resulted from men's growing power in a society that allowed them to interpret cultural elements to their and all men's advantage. In his paper "Conflict, Legitimacy and Tradition" in *Japanese Social Organization*, Theodore C. Bestor (1992, 24) uses the term "traditionalism" to describe that phenomenon; different groups in society implemented their interpretations or versions of local traditions to control social practices, lay claim to social status, and maintain or overturn the existing social order. In that context of traditionalism, men sought to exclude women from certain areas by imposing their interpretations of religious rules, including about women's impurity and *saké*'s jealous spirit. The framework of traditionalism also makes room for the case of Aizu Wakamatsu, which represents another interpretation, one opposed to existing ideas and allowed women to participate in *saké* production. Even so, the possibility cannot be ruled out that the exception in Aizu Wakamatsu was orchestrated by men, because women's labor was cheaper than men's, and poor economic circumstances prompted allowing women to engage in brewing *saké*.

In sum, the "unclean" women of the Tokugawa period, largely low in status and always lower in status than men, faced challenging cultural and economic circumstances that forced them to toil in the household and operate in society according to rules enforced by husbands and families. Ironically, although Christianity's arrival gave some women hope of finding a new identity by embracing a new faith, the new religion was also a patriarchal one.

The Arrival of Christianity in Japan

Women ranked among the earliest converts to Christianity in Japan and played an essential role in the Jesuit missions established in the nation during the Tokugawa period. By extension, a crucial factor of Christianity's growth during the era was women's active spreading of the Gospel, as well as the range of ministerial services that they offered, especially within Jesuit missions.

In late 16th-century Japan, Roman Catholics were called *Kirishitans*, derived from the word 'Christian,' and the first hundred years of Roman Catholic progress in Japan have thus been dubbed the "*Kirishitan* Century." Throughout that time, also called Japan's "Christian (Roman Catholic) Century," beginning with the arrival of Jesuits in 1549, Christianity took root and spread in Japan. In the mid-17th century, however, Christianity was banned in Japan, and Christians were thereafter persecuted until the collapse of the Tokugawa regime and the Meiji Restoration in 1868. For nearly two and a half centuries, Christians in Japan thus practiced their faith in secret as *Kakure Kirishitans*—that is, 'Hidden Christians.'

Upon landing in Japan in 1549, Francis Xavier (1506–1552) was welcomed with a friendly reception at Ijuin from one of the powerful lords of the land, Takahisa Shimazu (1514–1571) and, approved to preach Christianity and convert locals. The priest's sterling character was pivotal to his success—the lords and their ministers and influential monks were charmed by Xavier's charisma and strength—as well as by certain economic and political factors. Merchants and cargo ships, for example, followed the Jesuits throughout Japan, and the shoguns, like warlords, ensured that they profited from the commerce that ensued. Eager to proselytize in China, however, Xavier left Japan in 1551. During his two years in the country, Xavier oversaw the conversion of 1,000 Japanese and laid the foundation for the missionary work of the Jesuits who would replace him. He later wrote that, in many respects, the Japanese were superior to Europeans and referred to them as "the delight of my heart" (Boxer 1993, 40).

In cooperation with local Christians and their donation of lands and buildings, the Jesuits established several churches in Japan. Later, during the early period of Christian persecution, when the churches were destroyed or reclaimed by Buddhist priests and the city of Nagasaki was in the hands of civil authorities, many Japanese, especially Christians, offered shelter, food, and even donations to those in need. Such circumstances encouraged local Christian charities to cooperate directly with Jesuit priests and missionaries and practice their faith even despite the threat of persecution. Ward (2009, 11) has written that even though the Society of Jesus's constitution forbade members from routinely working with women or establishing a branch for them, women nevertheless performed apostolic activities such that "the ministry of women apostles characterized the Christian Century of Japan". Those women, as Ward (2009, 11) proposes, "created their own space of ministry beyond

Jesuit initiative in preaching, teaching, catechizing, religious debates, administration of certain sacraments, works of mercy for the poor, and martyrdom."

The First Christian Women in Japan

Christianity's arrival in Japan challenged the dominant Confucian view on the hierarchical position of women in society. Despite the patriarchalism of Roman Catholicism, Christianity offered unprecedented opportunities for women to discover and embody new social roles and positions in their newly found faith. In that process, they responded to and redefined their stance toward Shinto and Buddhist traditions and developed new ways of expressing religious identity (Ward 2009, 1).

Women gravitated toward Christianity for several reasons. Ward (2009) suggests that women were attracted to the faith because it promises salvation after death regardless of being a man or woman. Unlike the harsh conservative Buddhist views on women's afterlife, Christianity assured women of their and their loved ones' eternal life in paradise through prayer (Ward 2009, 12-13):

> While the orthodox Tendai and Shingon schools were on the decline in the late medieval period, the religious revivals among the more egalitarian "reformed" sects of Zen, Jōdo, Hokke, and Jōdo-Shinshū (or Ikkōshū) attracted women. All schools offered doctrines of the afterlife that offered little hope of women's salvation after death, however. The *ketsubonkyō* (blood bowl sutra) taught that because of the impurity due to their blood of menstruation and childbirth, all women must suffer in *ketsubon* (blood

lake) after death. Only if the firstborn sons recited *ketsubonkyō* for their mothers, may the mothers be rescued from the suffering.

Contrary to the "reformed" sects and perhaps in reaction to the growing number of Christian women in Japan, Kumano Bikuni Buddhism urged women to take their fate into their hands by reciting *ketsubonkyō* for themselves. Kumano Bikuni was a sect or order of Buddhist *bikuni* ('nuns') who traveled to Japan preaching about a Buddhist path to a positive afterlife for women.

The path to salvation for women offered by Kumano Bikuni, however, did not discourage some women in Japan from choosing Christianity instead, not only due to the promise of Christian salvation but because Christianity afforded women certain autonomy and motivated them to work with missionaries to care for people's well-being in this life. However, as Ward (2009, 15) writes:

> These demands of autonomy often placed women in danger. Christianity required women to make a personal decision about their religious choices and confess it publicly in a society where women's opinions mattered little. It required them to maintain a stronger loyalty to Christ than to their feudal lords, fathers, elder brothers, husbands, and sons. It empowered women to take vows of celibacy, or choose their marriage partners from among Kirishitan men.

Such loyalty to Christ endangered the patriarchal system on which Japanese society and culture were based. Those in power within that patriarchal network were also threatened by the choices that the women in their lives—their daughters, sisters, and wives—made not only to follow Christ but also move beyond their preset family contexts, clans, and social classes. Women mobilized to practice "leadership in ministries of teaching, persuading, preaching, and works of mercy" (Ward 2009, 15). Ward even suggests that the emancipation of *Kirishitan* women motivated the Tokugawa regime to begin persecuting Christians in Japan, which led to the martyrdom of many *Kirishitan* women and men during a nearly three-century ban on Christianity.

Women's conversion to Christianity was indeed based on their autonomous decision to follow Christ, not due to being compelled by their fathers, older brothers, husbands, or other superiors. Despite the custom that once the head of a shogunate converted to Christianity, the people under his protection would convert as well, such was not always the case with women. Some women chose Christianity even despite the objections and abuses of their husbands. As mentioned, women married into their husbands' families and were sometimes abused and often overburdened with duties and obligations. Choosing Christianity was thus a sign of protest and a path to liberation. As Ward (2009, 10) suggests, Christian women's conversions were authentic, sincere, and profound—the "fruit of years of maturation and struggle."

Kirishitan Women and Their Ministries

Women played various roles in spreading Christianity in Japan during the Tokugawa period— as translators, writers, teachers (e.g., catechists and apologists), debaters, speakers, evangelists, charity workers, and social advocates—at a time when women not only in Japan but also worldwide had few rights. In particular, women helped to contextualize and localize the message of the Gospel, especially as translators of Christian literature (Ward 2012, 221). Through their work, they helped in the domestication of Christian messages by reappropriating familiar keywords and expressions from Buddhism (Ward 2012, 63). Even so, as Ward (2009, 9) has observed, "No scholar has yet extensively considered the apostolic role which *Kirishitan* women leaders played in its social, religious, and historical context," partly because most Christian literature translated or written by Christians in Japan during the period was destroyed when Christianity was banned in 1612.

In the following paragraphs, I focus on women's spiritual and intellectual ministry (e.g., catechism) and the charity work that paralleled what we now call social activism. Even though many women conducted such spiritual and intellectual ministry, I have selected Gracia Tama Hosokawa (1563–1600) and Julia Naitō (1566–1627) as representative cases, while for charity work and social activism, I have chosen the example of Justa of Nagasaki (1563–?).

Women as Catechists

During Japan's Christian Century (1549–1650), women catechists explained Christian doctrines using the language and concepts of Buddhist traditions with which the Japanese were familiar (Ward 2009, 63). Hosokawa is an example of a scholarly woman who translated Catholic texts from Europe into Japanese, including the catechism and various spiritual treatises (Ward 2009, 206). Gifted in Japanese script, Gracia applied her talents to understand the new *Kirishitan* faith and contextualize Christianity, thereby making the new faith easier to understand and accept by local residents. By comparison, Julia Naitō was a pioneer in utilizing Japanese religious and cultural elements to debate and persuade Japanese Buddhists and Shinto followers to embrace Christianity. Naitō and several *Kirishitan* women also established the *Kirishitan* Women's Society, aka *Miyako no bikuni* ('Nuns of Miyako'), the only known women's "convent-like" organization in the Christian Century (Ward 2009, 61).

Gracia Tama Hosokawa

Gracia Tama Hosokawa, henceforth called simply "Gracia," was born in 1563. Her father, Mitsuhide Akechi, in the service of Nobunaga Oda, enjoyed a relatively strong financial position that enabled him to give all of his children a good education, including Gracia, which predominately focused on Zen Buddhism. Gracia's education prepared her to later become one of Japan's most famous *Kirishitan* theologians during the Tokugawa period and develop a love for intellectual discussions that spanned her entire life (Sander 2016, 1).

Gracia first encountered Christianity through her husband, Tadaoki, a noble samurai with several wives, amid a marital relationship full of tension. Tadaoki became acquainted with Ukon Takayama, a well-known Christian samurai in Japan at the time who tried to evangelize him. Although his conversion failed, Gracia learned about Christianity from her husband's reports. According to Sander (2016, 2), though Gracia became fascinated by Christianity, she attended church only once in her life. Barred from leaving her husband's palace in Osaka, she was unable to attend church except on one occasion, when she managed to flee the palace in secret and venture into a church. Although she immediately decided to be baptized upon hearing the sermon, doing so would have required her to reveal her identity. When the palace guards discovered Gracia's absence, located her, and brought her back, she was thereafter forbidden to attend church by her husband.

Nevertheless, her single visit to church radically changed the atmosphere of Tadaoki's palace, as several of his wives and other women there—17 women in total—converted to Christianity. Gracia and the other women, as a group generally isolated and left to themselves in the palace, led a nearly monastic life there, praying together and discussing philosophy and Christian literature. Gracia's best friend, Ito Kiyohara (aka Kojiju), renamed Maria after being baptized, served as the intermediary between Gracia and the priest in Osaka, relaying their questions and answers (Sander 2016, 3). In time, Gracia completed several written works and translations, including books on the catechism, although all of her *Kirishitan* writings and letters of inquiry to the priest have since been destroyed.

When Ieyasu Tokugawa (1543–1616) succeeded Hideyoshi Toyotomi (1537–1598) upon his death in 1598, various clans renounced the succession. Gracia's husband, Tadaoki, took the side of Ieyasu, who was also anti-Christian. Facing political unrest and the possibility of Gracia's being taken hostage, Tadaoki ordered her death. Although the 17 other Christian women at the palace wanted to die with her as well, they were prevented from doing so.[1] Sander (2016, 4) has proposed that Gracia died not in sacrifice for her religion but owing to her husband's political position; otherwise, she would not have prevented the other women

---

1 There are disagreements about Gracia's death. Some claim Gracia committed suicide on the orders of her husband. However, this is problematic since suicide is considered a sin in Christianity.

from receiving death because, as Christians, they also have a right to martyrdom. In this way, Gracia wanted to prevent more people from having to die for Tadaoki.

Julia Naitō

Julia Naitō, henceforth "Julia," an ordained nun and speaker, became known for her explanations of the catechism, Catholic beliefs and her public debates with Buddhist priests and scholars, including her former Buddhist master priest. According to Ward (2009, 63), Julia "continued to develop her method of religious disputation and persuasive conversations about differences between Christianity and Japanese religions to convert Japanese noblewomen and men."

Ward (2009, 64-66) suggests that Fabian Fukan (1565–1621), the spiritual director of the Kirishitan Women's Society *(Miyako no Bikuni)*, used Julia and her nuns as a model for Yūtei, a figure in the *Myotei Mondo* (1605), a standard Jesuit manual for women catechists by Fabian Fukan (1565–1621) or Habian Fukunsai, a prominent Jesuit apologist and public speaker. In *Myotei Mondo*, written as a dialogue between two women, both widowed by the war and former Buddhist nuns, Myōshū, a newcomer, asks theological questions of Yūtei, a confirmed Christian believer, who explains to her the truth of Christianity compared with other religions (Paramore 2009, 14). Thus, there is a strong probability that Yutei's apologetics recounted in *Myotei Mondo* was the same as Julia's and her nuns' in the Kirishitan Women's Society. Added to that, the character Myōshū is depicted as a nun of Pure Land Buddhism, a Japanese alternative to Roman Catholicism during the Tokugawa period, especially concerning salvation and paradise, whose doctrine is premised on the promise that those who call and recite the name of Amida will enter

Jōdo, the "Pure Land" and paradise. In *Myotei Mondo*, Myōshū indeed asks Yūtei questions concerning paradise. In response, as Ward (2009, 67) has described eloquently:

> Having refuted the Jōdo doctrine, Yūtei argues for the superiority of Christianity. She sees a clear difference between the certainty of Kirishitan Paraiso in heaven and the final nothingness of the Jōdo *paradise*. She underscores that in addition to this belief in the certain physical presence of heaven, Christianity gave its followers clearer knowledge of the afterlife. Throughout the Middle Ages, divination became a popular practice for people who wanted to know where their beloved dead wandered in the endless cycle of reincarnation. One was never sure about in which of the six worlds the spirit of the dead may arrive after death, although chances were that it would go to one of the four worlds of hell. There was another hell of *ketsubon* (blood lake), into which all women who failed ōjō (instant transport to Jōdo by reciting the name of Amida at the very moment of death) would fall because of their impurity in menstruation and childbirth. In contrast, Yūtei shows, there was no women-only hell in Christianity. Christianity does not view women as the sole source of human corruption but sees the source in men also. It was both Adan (Adam) and Ewa (Eve) who brought about the original sin, while it was the Virgin Mary who introduced the redemption of humankind by giving birth to Christ. Salvation in *Paraiso* is readily available for Kirishitan women. Thus, Yūtei explains to Myōshū, she only needs to "receive the sacrament

of baptism, keep the ten commandments, and worship God." Then "she would be peaceful in this life. And in the other life, she would live in *Paraiso*."

The fragment provides only a glimpse into the scholastic abilities in Christian theology of women such as Julia, which unfortunately eroded due to the patriarchal dynamics in which Christianity functioned. Nevertheless, Jesuits later acknowledged that Christianity's popularity and growth among women were due to the ministry of Julia, an expert debater, and evangelist who converted, baptized, and helped many women of noble status throughout Kyoto during the Tokugawa period (Ward 2009, 72).

Women of Charity

From 1467 to 1615, Japan was constantly in a state of civil war, experienced vast social and political turmoil, and witnessed attempts at national unification. The period from 1467 to 1615 is called the "Sengoku period," which literary means 'state of war.' As a result of those sources of volatility, women were victimized, as happens in every war and bout of civil unrest. According to Ward (2009, 295), "Women daily experienced precarious situations of war, violence, slavery, homelessness, dislocation, starvation, sickness, poverty, and being taken hostage." The Roman Catholic missionaries witnessed those atrocities against women, and gradually, as the number of Christians in Japan swelled, *Kirishitans*, especially women, mobilized in offering charity and social and spiritual care for women. Ward (2009, 295) has written of the "Kirishitan women of *confrarias* who led apostolic works of mercy," with "*confrarias*" referring to Christian volunteer associations within the Roman Catholic Church.[2]   Ward (2009, 305) has added that, according to Arimichi Ebisawa, a Japanese church historian, *confrarias* in Japan can be categorized into three types. The first, *Misericórdia*, between 1552–1614, provided direct assistance to the poor. The second type was represented by the Marian congregations (1614–1663), which taught moral values, united underground churches, and promoted zeal for martyrdom while preparing members for survival. The third type of charity ministry arose during the two centuries of Hidden Christianity during which *confrarias* helped *Kirishitans* survive the ban on Christianity for 200 years without clergy (Ward 2009, 305). In those groups, women charity workers offered services in children's ministry, provided medical care, and performed rituals such as burials and baptisms.

Justa of Nagasaki

Justa of Nagasaki was the founder of the Confraternity of Mercy in Nagasaki, the Consorority of Married Sisters, and the Confraria of Mercy in Yatsushiro, to name only a few of the remarkable organized works of charity that she offered to *Kirishitans* in Japan, especially to women (Ward 2009, 295). By the late 16th century, the city of Nagasaki had become an essential port in Japan as a commercial harbor for foreigners from different parts of the world. Because Nagasaki's lord *(daimyō)*, Bartolomeu Sumitada Ōmura, allowed Jesuits to practice their missionary work in his ports, Nagasaki also became a center for Christians in Japan. Even *Kirishitans*

---

2 A *confraternity* (Spanish: *cofradía*; Portuguese: confraria) is generally a Christian voluntary association of lay people created to promote exceptional works of Christian charity or piety and approved by the Church hierarchy.

who were persecuted elsewhere in the nation found refuge in Nagasaki and its surrounding areas (Ward 2009, 296). In that setting, two laypeople—Justa and her husband, Justino, a carpenter and goldsmith—initiated works of charity to serve the church and people in need (Ward 2009, 300).

Misericórdia in Nagasaki was exceptional in its day for having a woman, Justa, as its founder and leader. Justa and her husband, who helped churches to be built in Nagasaki and elsewhere (e.g., Kyoto), invested vast sums of money in the ministry of charity work (Ward 2009, 299). Justa was an independent woman and at times made decisions and implemented them without receiving the requisite prior consent of the priests. For example, she appointed married women to service in charity work without asking permission from the priests of Nagasaki. She also established rules for the Sisters of Charity and for the House of Charity and only afterward informed the priests (Ward 2009, 302). Justa also managed a nursing home for women that developed into a more extensive operation with two hospitals—one for women and one for men—in addition to the original leprosarium (Ward 2009, 303). Ward (2009, 303) has thus observed the spirit of women's activism and Christian feminism in the figure of Justa:

> It is important to note that, unlike the Portuguese Misericórdia, the gender role was reversed in Nagasaki. It was Justa, a woman, who wrote the rules and guided administrative decisions in her "board" of 12 sisters of the Consorority, like the *mesa*. The board then supervised other women, who provided the works of mercy to poor women and men in the nursing home and community.

In short, women contributed tremendously to charity and activism in Tokugawa society even during the two and half centuries of Hidden Christianity. They aided widows and orphans and offered shelter to abused women who had escaped or divorced their husbands. Their charitable works gradually turned into activism to support *Kakure Kirishitans* despite the risks of punishment that awaited them if they were caught practicing the Christian faith.

The Persecution of Christians in Tokugawa Society

As described earlier, "There was a direct link between this proliferation of Kirishitan women's apostolic ministries and the radicalization of Japanese political ideology in the first half of the seventeenth century" (Ward 2009, 15). Ward suggests that by accepting neo-Confucianism as a state ideology in 1607, the Tokugawa shogunate's ambition was to create a stratified society with a separation of class and gender. As a result of that ideological change, Japan ultimately rejected Christianity and reverted to the oppression of religion and women in society for centuries to come.

In the early Tokugawa period, the ministry of *Kirishitan* women attained certain independence and flourished. However, because such independence was unacceptable within the ideological boundaries of neo-Confucianism and state rules, the ministry, given its resistance and opposition to the oppression of *Kirishitan* women, was also unacceptable to the patriarchal neo-Confucian leaders of the Tokugawa regime. As a result, in 1614, the Tokugawa regime declared Julia Naitō and her Kirishitan Women's Society a political threat and exiled them to Manila in the Philippines. In time, the Tokugawa regime decided to wholly eradicate Christianity from Japan, and any person found practicing the Christian faith was to be tortured, publicly disgraced, and eventually put to death.

The persecution of Christians in the Tokugawa period is divided into two eras. In the early period, persecution commenced beginning with the martyrdom of 26 believers in 1597, followed by periodical public executions of Christians, including women and children. Those sporadic acts of persecution became more systematic in 1637 with the suppression of the Shimabara Rebellion led by a young Kirishitan man named Shirō Amakusa (1621–1638). Although the revolt was driven by economic and political grievances against the government, the Tokugawa administration mistook it for a religiously-motivated insurrection because its commander was a Kirishitan.

By 1640, *Kirishitan Shumon aratame-yaku* ('Christian Suppression Office'), established to systematically persecute Christians, had developed strategies for locating Hidden Christians and established a bounty system to incentivize people to report Christians to the regime. Among its tactics was making all Japanese residents become Buddhists and forcing them to register their names in local or regional Buddhist temples or else be executed. Another means of identifying and persecuting Christians was *e-fumi* ceremonies, in which Japanese were regularly obliged to trample on a sacred Christian symbol (e.g., a cross or an image of Christ or the Virgin Mary) or else be put to death. During the ceremonies, Christian women would show signs of heavy emotion and even break out into a sweat, and even while trampling on the symbols, they secretly showed reverence to them. If the observing official suspected anyone of deception, they were punished as well.

In 1614, when the persecution of Christians began in full force, there were nearly one million Christians in Japan. According to Drummond (1971, 72) in *A History of the Christian Church in Japan*, Christianity was organized "in a manner similar to the church in the Roman Empire, a single church consisted of distinct groups in a relatively extended geographical area." This made Christianity become the largest single organized religious community within the nation at the time. By 1635, although, about 280,000 Christians had been executed (Hagemann 1942), although other sources claim that this figure includes not only executions but also starvation and poverty, which were also indirect effects of the persecution.

Women, alongside men, were persecuted, tortured, and killed for their faith in Christ. In *Japan's Martyr Church*, Sister Mary Bernard (1926, 84) has described how

> Men, women, and children of every age and rank were tied naked into sacks filled with sharp straws and other wounding substances. Carried about thus, and exposed to the jeers of the mob, they were thrown aside in huddled-up heaps, and after exposure to the winter, cold were burnt in piles. Many were tortured before death by the insertion of sharp spikes under the nails of their hands and feet, whilst some poor wretches by a refinement of horrid cruelty were shut up in cages and there left to starve with food before their eyes.

In the single decade from 1619 to 1628, scores of women from Japan were recognized by the Catholic Church as martyrs—to name a few, Joannes Yoshida Shōun, Magdalena Kiyota Bokusai, Maria Gengorō, Agnes Takeya, Apollonia of

Nagasaki, Catharina of Nagasaki, Isabella Fernandes, Clara Yamada, Maria Tanaka, Lucia de Freitas, Magdalena Sanga, Maria Hamanomachi, Maria Murayama, Maria Tanaura, Maria Yoshida, Thecla Nagaishi, Lucia Yakichi, Catharina Tanaka, Monica Onizuka, Zuzanna Araki Chobyōe, Magdalena Kiyota, Maria Vaz or Maria Shōbyōe, and Lucia Ludovica. Although the exact number of *Kirishitan* women who died for their faith remains unknown, it likely reached a few thousand during the Tokugawa period.

Kakure Kirishitans: Hidden Christians

Kakure Kirishitans were the descendants of the brave women and men of Japan who practiced Christianity in secret and organized an underground church during the more than 250-year period of persecution from 1614 until 1873. Throughout those two centuries of the underground church and its total lack of priests, the Christian message that was once preached and practiced by missionaries during Japan's Christian Century gradually changed to a radical degree. Individuals who initially practiced the Christian faith underground could probably not clearly distinguish Christianity from Buddhism, and that ambiguity doubtlessly intensified over the prolonged course of covert practice. In many ways, *Kakure Kirishitans* thus unintentionally wove together Buddhist cosmology and Christian mythology. During the period of the underground church, women played an essential role by passing on to their children what they had learned from their ancestors.

In 1858, some years after Commodore Matthew Perry arrived in his "Black Ship" and signed the U.S.–Japan Treaty of Amity and Commerce, Americans were allowed to practice Christianity, and similar agreements with other countries permitted foreign missionaries from other countries to practice their faith there as well. The doors thus reopened for the Catholic Church to return to Japan and resume its work, which would come to include the establishment of churches in Hakodate, Yokohama, Edo (in present day Tokyo), and Nagasaki.

On March 17, 1865, Father Bernard Petitjean, a priest of the French Societé des Missions Etrangères, heard a noise at the back door of his newly established chapel on the Ōura slope in Nagasaki. Upon opening the door, he was surprised to find a group of 15 middle-aged Japanese men and women who claimed to be members of the Hidden Christian community. Three women then knelt beside him, said, "The heart of all of us here is the same as yours," and asked, "Where is the statue of Maria-Sama?" (Marnas 1896, 488). Although Father Petitjean encouraged the *Kakure Kirishitans* of Urakami to practice their faith openly because Christianity remained outlawed, his new flock paid a harsh price for his enthusiasm; 3,404 were arrested, some were tortured, and many were put to death. It was only in 1873 that, under intense pressure from abroad, Japan's anti-Christian edict became defunct (Marnas 1896, 270).

In 1868, the collapse of the Tokugawa regime gave way to the Meiji period (1868–1912), when a new, young Japan sought to modernize its political, social, economic, cultural, and religious systems, in which women came to play an important role in Japanese society, including as Christians during and beyond the Meiji period.

WOMEN & CHRISTIANITY

in the Meiji Period, 1868 - 1912

Chapter Two

WOMAN & CHRISTIANITY
in the Meiji Period, 1868 - 1912

With the Meiji Restoration in 1868, Japanese society embraced a new vision for the country's future, including for women, although not necessarily with any improvement in their social status. On the contrary, women's new role was in Japan's industrialization, as cheap laborers to support the process of developing a strong, prosperous nation. The transformation from feudalism to an industrial capitalist society in Japan prompted demonstrations and strikes as well as unleashed various diseases such as cholera. Those trends also affected the position and role of women in Japan, out of which the principles of women's movements opposing the tragedy of women's status in Japan were born. The changes concerning women's role and status in Meiji society can be better analyzed by first reviewing a brief historical background of the period.

In 1868, the newly established government in Japan, the Meiji regime, launched an ambitious program to turn Japan into a modern, centralized national state reflecting the Western European model but even better economically and military-wise than Western European countries. With the objective of *fukoku kyohei*, meaning a prosperous country and strong army, *oitsuki oikose*, or catching up and surpassing the West, was the mantra that summed up the new government policy.

The central figures within the new government came from groups that had made themselves creditable in the fight against the restoration of imperial rule. The nine leaders in total, including five from the samurai class and called *genro* (i.e., old oligarchic group of elders during the Meiji period), agreed that Japan was a weak, poor, backward country able to survive only by navigating the actions of aggressive imperialist nations. The new regime's primary financial basis was a land tax, which in the first decade of the Meiji period accounted for 80% to 90% of all government revenue. The government capitalized the land, and an assessment was made of each plot to determine the tax owed, to be paid annually in cash. Some smallholder farmers could not meet those requirements, which led to the creation of a group of rural capitalists and large landowners whose smallholders leased their land. In supporting the new processes designed to revolutionize Japan, women worked exceptionally hard and were typically exploited.

The most crucial step of the Meiji reform was to industrialize Japan following the Western model, with an emerging class of industrialists, as Peter Worsley (1964, 130) has described:

> Here [in Japan] the ruling classes in an agrarian feudal society—though one which possessed a significant urban and commercial sector even before the arrival of the Commodore Perry—were able to come to terms with modern capitalism by investing heavily in the new industrial economy which was rapidly constructed after the Meiji Restauration. The result was a peculiarly centralized and concentrated pattern of political control and economic ownership, in which indigenous finance capital was closely

interlinked with industrial enterprise, but where older feudal-paternalist traditions persisted and affected relations between management and workers. From this launching platform, Japan successfully built up a modern capitalist economy.

In describing the brutal "train" of development, Worsley identifies the ruling classes as the first industrialists, meaning that their preexisting ideas about hierarchy, the position of women, and social norms would guide Japan's industrialization. Worsley also observes that the highly centralized, concentrated patterns of political control and industrial companies acted as vessels to preserve old feudal paternalistic traditions. For the status of women, that harsh context of industrialization and capitalism had unclear implications.

Women in Meiji Society

Ideas about modernization during the Meiji Restoration precipitated significant changes. In 1872, influenced by Western enlighteners, a civil rights movement emerged to abolish human trafficking, a dirty trade that endangered women, including servants and prostitutes. Showcasing the evils of trafficking women was the *Maria Lutz* affair, named after a Peruvian ship that took men and women from Asia to other parts of the world, where the men were sold as laborers and women as prostitutes and maids.

Another significant change, one that arguably formed the basis for subsequent emancipation movements, was the implementation of general compulsory education on September 5, 1872, which gave women and men equal rights to pursue education. Whether the new actually succeeded in providing equal opportunities for men and women, however, is doubtful. In the countryside, the family head, usually a man, allowed girls to attend school but only to learn sensible, typically feminine subjects. According to Meyvis and Vande Walle (1989, 143), women began to count at the level of the family only after Japan had resolutely moved toward industrial development.

Meiji society hovered between the feudal norms and values of the Tokugawa period and the new modern ideas coming from the West. As a consequence, society as a whole did not know how to approach various social problems, including women's rights. Whereas some believed that women should remain as they were in Tokugawa society, Japan wanted to advance toward becoming a modern society, an effort that women could support. According to Sievers (1983), although Meiji leaders, primarily of the samurai class, preferred to maintain women's positions as they had been in Tokugawa society, doing so was impossible under Western eyes that criticized Japan for violating women's rights.

Nevertheless, Meiji leaders sought to exclude women by way of various measures. In 1872, the Meiji government founded the Tokyo Girls School; however, in 1877, after only five years in operation, the school was inexplicably forced to close (Sievers 1983, 11). More generally, women were often exploited as cheap laborers in the processes of industrialization. A prime example of women's discrimination was the Iwakura Mission, beginning in 1871, when the government sent students, including five women, to the United States for a study stay of 10 years. Upon returning, the young men obtained decent jobs in government agencies, whereas no one in the Meiji government could explain why the women, who never received jobs, had been sent abroad in the first place. On the topic, Sievers (1983, 13) has written that:

> In terms of women's education, the decision to send the five girls with the Iwakura mission had little or no impact. But it did produce some benefits in terms of Japan's image in the West, and it continued to be used in later years as a convenient example of Japan's progressive attitude toward women in speeches and articles intended for Western consumption.

One of those five women, Umeko Tsuda (1864–1929), later became an important figure in higher education for women in Japan, as discussed later in this chapter.

The Iwakura Mission was not the first Japanese mission to send locals to the United States and Europe, for as early as 1860, students were going on missions to the United States. Such missions played a decisive role in raising awareness about women's situation in Japan relative to other countries. Women ventured to the West and returned confused, having witnessed just how much more freedom Western women enjoyed than their counterparts in Japan. They saw, for example, that women were allowed to walk alongside their husbands in public, which was strictly prohibited in samurai culture. They also saw how Western women did not simply perform household chores but played a leadership role in the domestic sphere. Although most participants in the 1860 mission nevertheless left the United States critical of the place that American women seemed to occupy in society, they recognized that American women were less demure and more assertive than women in Japan (Sievers 1983, 2). In time, Meiji leaders and scholars wondered whether Japan's underdevelopment compared with Western powers could be related to women's traditional status rooted in Tokugawa values.

Westernization also affected how men and women presented themselves in society. When the samurai hairstyle was replaced with a more closely cropped hairstyle, the new hairstyle aroused the interest of urban women who also began to cut their hair short. The Meiji government refused to allow women to sport the new look, however, and the short hairstyle was banned for women in 1872. In protest, some leaders of the women's movement continued to cut their hair short, and some were arrested. According to Sievers (1983), the introduction of the new hairstyle marked the beginning of women's attempts to join the progressive forces of society and, in turn, create a new Japan. The government's denial of their right to do so was also its denial of their right to participate and contribute actively to such progress and, in Sievers's (1983, 15) words, "a symbolic message to Japan's women to become repositories of the past, instead of pioneers, with men, of some unknown future."

At such a crucial point in choosing how to adopt a new policy for women, Meiji leaders opted for a dubious solution. On the one hand, they obliged women to be educated by law; on the other, they proved, often for mysterious reasons— for example, as in the closure of Tokyo Girls School—that the laws concerning woman's freedom were nothing than words on paper. Thus, women often became a cheap source of industrial labor for various factories, including for silk spinning, textiles, and mining. Industrialization brought workers homes, slums, sickness, and chaos, and in those miserable conditions, women earned only 30% of what men did, and roughly a quarter of the workers had to work at night (Meyvis and Vande Walle 1989, 143).

Various debates arose in the Meiji government regarding the position of women in Japan, and various questions were asked. For one, what should society expect from a woman in Japan? For another, what should education for women look like? How much education was enough, and what would distinguish it from that of men? Or would raising women's status per se lead to universally defined civilization and development? In relatively little time, the debate about women became a much-discussed topic nationally, and ideas about the status of women became sharply divided. The leading group concerned with women's rights was the *Meirokusha* ('Meiji Six Society'), named after the sixth year of the Meiji era, in which the group originated. *Meirokusha* thinkers were intellectuals who sought to contextualize Western ideas in the Japanese milieu, and three of them, all men, were intensively involved in contemplating the situation of women in Japan. Citing how the West continued to sharply criticize women's treatment in Japan, those three intellectuals believed that the effect was an attitude among Westerners that Japan was an underdeveloped society. The intellectuals—Arinori Mori (1847–1889) and Masanao Nakamaru (1832–1891), both influenced by Christianity, and Yukichi Fukuzawa (1835–1901)—claimed that women's treatment in Japan was indeed barbaric. In the *Meirokusha* magazine, *The Meiji Six Journal*, Fukuzawa wrote:

> Someone may counter that if a man supports a number of mistresses, there will be no violation of human nature if he treats them properly. This is the opinion of the man himself . . . If . . . true, a woman

should be allowed to support a number of husbands. She should be able to call them male concubines and give them lower-ranking positions in the household. ... By nature's decree, the number of male and female births seem about equal ... Accordingly, it is clearly against the law of nature when one husband has two or three wives. We should not hesitate to call such men beasts. (Sievers 1983, 20)

Convinced that women would inevitably be central in Japan's social progress, *Meirokusha* thinkers such as Mori and Fukuzawa were prominent figures in raising awareness for women's movements in Japan.

Women's Movements

The first women's movements in Japan—for example, the Women's Temperance Association, the counterpart of Western organizations such as the Women's Christian Temperance Union—were influenced primarily by Christianity, which opposed the country's legal prostitution trade. The most important movement was Jiyu Minken Undo, under the leadership of Taisuke Itagaki, which started, as mentioned below, originally for men in the 1880s. Well-known women of the movement include Toshiko Kishida (1863–1901) and Hideko Fukuda (1865–1927). Fukuda's persuasive speeches inspired Kishida to mobilize women in Japan. Hearing arguments that women were equal to men and must have equal rights in Japan's development, Fukuda became the great admirer of Kishida and joined the Popular Rights movement.

The Popular Rights movement was initiated in 1873 by several disaffected samurai who attempted to organize a rebellion against the government to restore the status of ex-samurai in Japan's new society. At first, the movement was controlled by men, such that the subject of women and their position was never discussed. In 1877, in Kyushu, the movement organized a rebellion against the government and emerged triumphant. As a result of the victory, the Popular Rights movement decided to operate no longer through uprisings but via politics, which led to the birth of the Liberal Party, the first political party in Japan.

In 1878, the Party's supporters increased, especially with farmers and traders, as the movement distanced itself from its exclusively pro-samurai origins. In that context, women had significant potential for the further development of the movement. Debates on gender and voting rights gradually surfaced, and in particular, a letter written by a housekeeper, Kita Kusunose (1836–1920), a 45-year-old woman from Hiroshima, redirected the debate about women's rights and the role of women in the Popular Rights movement. A month after the Hiroshima elections, Kusunose wrote a fiery letter about property rights, voting rights, and gender to the government. When the letter was widely circulated in the press, forcing the leaders of the Popular Rights movement to take it seriously, women and women's concerns began to play an essential part in the movement and the Liberal Party. A piece of Kusunose's letter reads as follows:

> We women who are heads of households must respond to the demands of the government just as other ordinary heads of households, but because we are women, we do not enjoy equal rights. We have the right neither to vote for district assembly representatives nor to act as legal guarantors in

matters of property, even though we hold legal instruments for that purpose. This is an enormous infringement of our rights! . . . If it is reasonable to assume that rights and duties go together, then we should make that widely held assumption that they are corresponding responsibilities a reality . . . I do not have the right to vote. I do not have the right to act as a guarantor. My rights, compared with those of male heads of households, are ignored. Most reprehensible of all, the only equality I share with men who are heads of their households is the onerous duty of paying taxes . . .

Officials to whom I complained tell me that men have greater rights than women because they bear the additional burden of military service . . . but my protest stands since it is well known that men are routinely excused from military service precisely because they are heads of their households! (Sievers 1983, 29)

Kusunose's letter brought about a conscious redirection of the discussions concerning women's rights. In 1881, a 16-year-old girl in Kyushu organized a conference on women's legislation in Japan, and in 1882, Kishida got involved in the Popular Rights movement and piqued the attention of its leaders at the movement's gathering in Osaka. A skilled speaker, Kishida became wildly popular all over the country as she traveled across Japan for various speeches and gatherings (Sievers 1983, 36).

The topics raised and arguments made by Kishida closely resembled those of women's movements in the West: equal access to education for women and equal sexual standards and civil rights for women as well. However, to that end, men first needed to reassess women's value in society and counter ancient teachings and customs purporting women as an evil that would make the people of any free civilized nation ashamed. Of them, the most reprehensible was the practice of respecting men and despising women. Despite cooperative efforts to build a new society, men in Japan continued to be respected as masters and husbands, whereas women were held in contempt as maids or servants. Because equality in such an environment is impossible, certain customs and traditions had to be dissolved, Kishida argued (Sievers 1983, 38), and women and men had to be equal in Japan's new society.

In Kishida's view, the inferior position of women in traditional Japan was not a consequence of gender but the result of an old patriarchal system that prevented women's access to education. Kishida believed that education was a necessary factor in raising the status of women in Japan and that the failed attempt at equal education in the Meiji period did not stem from the family's attitude toward women but misguided policies endorsed by the Meiji government concerning women. Kishida also spoke to Japanese parents to warn them that their daughters' future was in their hands:

> I hope in the future there will be some recognition of the fact that the first requirement for marriage is education. Today, we have come to feel that we have "managed" if eight out of ten daughters who are married do not return home in a divorce. No one should make such a claim. One of the first require-ments ought to be learning what it is to manage after marriage . . . Daughters must be taught basic economics and the skills that would permit them to

manage on their own. Even a woman who expects to be protected during her husband's lifetime must be able to manage on her own, armed with the necessary skills, if he should die. (Sievers 1983, 40)

At the same time, most of Kishida's criticism was directed at Japanese parents, who typically sought to protect their daughters by enforcing traditional rules and keeping them at home. Even when their daughters did attend school, they learned how to make floral decorations and organize tea ceremonies. According to Kishida, parents thus placed their daughters in an "invisible box" in which they had no room to grow (Sievers 1983, 41).

In 1889, the Liberal Party gradually began to disintegrate and officially disbanded in 1894. The Popular Rights movement continued, however, and immediately after the Party's dissolution, another party, the Imperial Party, announced the creation of Joshi Konshinkai ('Women's Friendship Society'). Thus, although the Popular Rights movement arguably did not directly alter Japanese politics, it ushered in a significant change in women's consciousness in Japan, which had been trapped within the traditional confines of samurai ethics for years. The movement thus gave rise to the conscious woman in Japan: a woman who started to wonder about her position in Japanese society, who started to write letters in protest, and who became active in politics. In that process of awareness, Kishida played an extraordinary, unforgettable role.

The Bluestockings

After the Popular Rights movement, various other movements emerged, some of which had Christian roots, whereas others were more concerned with socialist ideologies. The

Women Socialist Party, with its socialist background, and the Bluestockings, with its feminist ideology, exemplify those trends. *Bluestocking* (Seitô) is the name of a magazine in which influential Japanese feminist writers debated *atarashii onna* ('the new woman'). *Bluestocking* was founded by writer Raichō Hiratsuka (1886–1971) in September 1911 and began publishing work by writers such as Akiko Yosano (1878–1942), whose feminist ideas infused her arguments for equal rights, equal education, and equal developmental opportunities for women in Japan.

Another writer, socialist Kikue Yamakawa (1890–1980), wrote about the socialist view of history, according to which the system of private property, which it aimed to destroy, was responsible for the oppression of women. Even founder Hiratsuka wrote articles to demand priority and unique opportunities for mothers in society. Although all of those writers have been prominent figures in the history of the women's movement in Japan, the ideas of Yosano and her theory of the "new woman" merit special attention.

Yosano was the first child of a candy-store owner in Sakai. Her father had wanted a son as a first child, however, so Yosano was banned until her first brother was born (Rodd 1991, 179). Despite her father's extreme strictness, she was able to receive an education, finished high school, and quietly began composing poetry for publication in local magazines. She soon met Hiratsuka and began publishing her poems about women in *Bluestocking*, the first of which came to symbolize the feminist movement:

The Day the Mountains Move

The day the mountains move has come.
I speak but no one believes me.
For the time that the mountains have been asleep
But long ago they all danced with fire.
It doesn't matter if you believe this,
My friends, as long as you believe:
All the sleeping women
are now awake and moving.[1]

Decades later, in 1985, the poem would be read in Nairobi at the UN Commemoration Meeting for the International Year of Women (Rodd 1991, 180).

In 1912, *Bluestocking* began to publish a series of articles about the "new woman" in which Yosano participated. The central theme of the articles was the protection of mothers and children by the government. Yosano was inspired by South African author Olive Schreiner, the author of *Woman and Work*, which was translated into Japanese in 1914. Schreiner demanded not only government support for women but also women's economic independence. About Schreiner's ideology, Yosano defended the economic independence of women and argued that a good marriage had to be based on the economic independence of women and men. That ideology was found to be intriguing not only by elite women but also by the women from proletarian families (Molony 1993, 127).

Yosano opposed the ideas of Leo Tolstoy and Ellen Key, that "It was the natural selection of the man who had to do the heavy physical and mental work (Rodd 1991, 189)." Yosano's

---

1 "The Day the Mountains Move," was first published in *Seitô* in 1911.

46

ideas and criticism of Key especially sparked a split in Japan's women's movement. One group believed that motherhood was women's original work, that the world of women is restricted to their family, and that without a woman, the family means nothing. The other group, Yosano's supporters, were convinced that women, as fellow humans alongside men, should have the same rights and the absolute freedom to act as men do.

Despite many debates between intellectuals and various articles in *Bluestocking* about the new woman, the Japanese government continued to occupy itself with other affairs, including building up the country's arms industry, countering domination by the West, and preparing for war and the world of imperialism. Although the government seemed to have little time to listen to women's criticisms, it desperately needed the cheap labor of women in various factories: the hard-working women who had to sacrifice themselves to the whims of the Japanese government and the illusions of modernization that they sustained. Thus, whereas women such as Yosano dreamed of a society where women have the right to protect themselves from poverty, unfair wages, illness, and the difficulties of pregnancy, the men of the Japanese government planned to see Asia conquered by Japan.

As the cogs of war ramped up worldwide, Yosano and other feminists continued to fight for a society with equal rights and new opportunities for women in Japan. Although Yosano, who died in 1942, did not see the end of World War II, other feminists in the *Bluestocking* wrote, discussed, and organized in postwar Japan.

Christianity in the Meiji Period

As mentioned, during the Meiji period, as Japan opened its borders to the outside world, many aspects of life in the country began to change, including the situation for Christians. During the period, especially after the introduction of new laws about religion in 1873, Christianity became officially tolerated in Japan, and Protestant Christianity arrived in the country, where it emerged in the form of Meiji Protestantism as a result of the Meiji Restoration. Nevertheless, because Christianity was still regarded as a foreign faith and was strongly associated with Western colonization, Japanese authorities were cautious in their dealings with Christians. When Protestant missionaries first arrived in Japan in 1859, they were initially restricted to a few large cities, and the Japanese continued to be prohibited from becoming Christians.

Protestantism entered Japan via two channels. The first was through Western church agencies and mission boards who sent missionaries to the island nation, the first of whom arrived in 1859. They were not invited but ventured to and stayed in Japan on their initiative. As for the second channel, Protestants from overseas were offered employment by Japanese agencies, including Reverend G. F. Verbeck, a missionary long employed by the Japanese government as an advisor in various capacities. Several other Protestants who arrived in Japan as government-employed instructors also profoundly influenced Protestant history (Lande 1989, 36).

As the Christian population grew in Japan, converts in the period came to be classified into two groups: samurai converts and converts from the farming class. Most early Protestant converts were from the samurai class, which was relatively open to Christianity because their children had attended Western schools and because they had more contact with Westerners than others in Japan. They also had access to Chinese-language Bibles, and some had even already read them (Lande 1989, 43). Similar to samurai, farmers were hungry for modern knowledge and adopted new lifestyles suited to the demands of the changing world.

Modernization and Christianity

Regarding the path Japan should take in modernization, a majority of Japan's intellectuals put their faith in Western technology while a minority believed that Japan should be modernized through Christianity. Among Japanese intellectuals who strongly promoted Christianity and its application to the situation in Japan, Joseph (Jo) Hardy Neesima (1843–1890) was from the samurai class, had converted to Christianity, and subsequently studied theology in the United States. Upon returning to Japan with a dream to modernize Japan by way of the Christian faith, Neesima founded the Doshisha School, which later became a well-regarded university. Other Christians in Japan also directly or indirectly supported the modernization of Japan in various areas such as education, and missionaries were either invited to Japan or came of their own accord to educate children and youth in languages and sciences. Because those teachers had the opportunity to share their faith with the future generation of the Japanese population, they and their schools exerted significant influence on society.

Women and Christianity in Meiji Japan

Unlike Roman Catholic missions of the late 16th century, missionaries during the Meiji period included women, who ventured to Japan to contribute to advancing the Gospel in the newly opened, modernizing nation. Between 1859 and 1869, Episcopal, Reformed, and Presbyterian Mission Boards sent American missionaries and their wives to Japan, and by 1882, 56 unmarried women and 81 wives were on their staff. Kohiyama (1992, 186–87) has observed that if wives are counted, about two-thirds of all foreign Protestant missionaries sent to Japan from 1859 to 1882 were women. Although the men among the missionaries dominated decision-making, women played an important role at the grassroots level. The wives of missionaries presented practical evidence of Christian family life in their daily lives, and they usually participated in missionary work themselves, to a greater or lesser degree (Ballhattchet 2007, 180). Many mission schools also taught girls English, with the Bible as a textbook, as well as Western culture (Howe 1995, 84). Thus, Christian women, both foreign missionaries and native Japanese, exerted increasing influence on Japanese society. Many women's groups—large and small, national and local, Christian, and non-Christian—were socially active in evangelization, social work, human rights advocacy for women, and securing women's right to education.

The following paragraphs provide only a glimpse into the contributions of Christian women to Japanese society, beginning with the arrival of women missionaries in Japan. Women missionaries inspired and trained native Christian women in the country who would later impact the nation with the Gospel and advocacy for women's rights and education.

The Women of the Iwakura Mission

Women's higher education in Japan is arguably rooted in the Iwakura Mission, in which Christian women played a crucial role. The Iwakura Mission, a series of Japanese diplomatic visits to the United States and Europe between 1871 and 1873, was initially proposed by Guido Verbeck (1830–1898), a Dutch missionary, educator, and one of the most influential foreign political advisors in the Meiji government. The Mission's delegation consisted of prominent diplomats and scholars tasked with gaining diplomatic recognition of the newly installed imperial dynasty and reexamining, redefining, and renegotiating existing treaties between Japan and Western powers.

Initially, the Meiji government sent more than a hundred personnel with the Iwakura Mission, including embassy members and 43 government students, some of whom were girls and women. Sent to learn about the United States and Europe in the fields of education, science, technology, political science, and military structures, the women students of the Mission were quite young. The oldest was Teiko Ueda and Ryōko Yoshimasu, both 15 or 16 years old, while younger ones included Princess Sutematsu Ōyama (11 or 12 years old), Shigeko Nagai (10 years old), and Umeko Tsuda (6–9 years old).[2] The Empress Shōken (1849–1914)[3] hoped that the young women would bring back methods from abroad that were needed to promote and modernize women's education in Japan.

---

2   Due to controversy about the age of the participants, I have indicated only an approximate age.

3   Empress Shōken was one of the founders of the Japanese Red Cross Society.

However, within a few years, the Meiji government shifted its stance on women's status in society. As Tsuda, one of the Mission's women, later revealed, although the five women sent from Japan were students of government and trained as teachers, they never received any jobs from the Japanese government upon their return (Shibahara 2010, 224–225). Instead, the Meiji government endorsed another path for women: that of the "good wife, wise mother," known in Japanese as *ryōsai-kenbo*, who is submissive, obedient, and self-sacrificing. Such a woman would obey her father when she was young, her husband when she married, and her son when she was old. The idea of *ryōsai-kenbo* was implemented in Meiji educational policies and resulted in the Meiji Civil Code of 1898, which affirmed the man as the head of the family and stipulated that all legal contracts, marriages, and divorces involving women had to be approved by men as the heads of their households. Only in 1945, after Japan's surrender to the Allied Forces, was the Meiji Civil Code of 1898 abolished.

Once again, the destiny of women was determined by a patriarchal institution that had oppressed women for generations. However, that adversity did not deter women as the train of growth and progress chugged onward, and as women increasingly seized control of their destiny, they promoted women's rights and equality in education. In that process, Christianity was an indispensable ally of women, one that played an important role, beginning with the women of the Iwakura Mission. Two of those women were devout Christians—Nagai and Tsuda, who later determined the fate of women's education and rights in Japan.

Umeko Tsuda

Umeko Tsuda (1864-1929) was the youngest girl among the members of the Iwakura Mission. Born in the Ushigome District of Edo, in present-day Minami Shinjuku of Tokyo Tsuda arrived in San Francisco in 1871 no more than 10 years old and lived in the United States as a student until she was 18. Upon returning to Japan as a devoted Christian, she became a pioneer in women's education in the Meiji period. On July 19, 2019, *Tokyo Weekender* published the results of a survey on the most prominent Japanese women, and Tsuda ranked within the top 20. In 2024, she will appear on the ¥5,000 bill.[4]

In the United States, Tsuda lived with Charles Lanman, the secretary of the Japanese legation, and Adeline Lanmans, both of whom were committed Episcopalians. Inspired by their faith, Tsuda also embraced Christianity and was baptized. After her studies abroad, she returned to Japan in 1882, where she worked as a tutor for children. Her time back home was short, for she soon returned to the United States to pursue a college education at Bryn Mawr College in Philadelphia, where she majored in biology and education.

Tsuda became convinced that the only way to improve women's status in Japan was to give them the same opportunity to enter higher education as men. Therefore, during her second stay in the United States, she established a scholarship fund, the American Scholarship for Japanese Women, to aid women in Japan in studying in the United States and returning to their motherland in becoming leading

---

4   https://www.tokyoweekender.com/2019/07/who-is-the-greatest
    -japanese-woman-ever/

forces in developing and improving women's education in Japan. Tsuda's fund helped many women in Japan study in the United States and some of them later became influential political and educational leaders in Japan during and after the Meiji period.

Tsuda continued advocating for women's education because the existing school for girls and women aimed only to educate them to be submissive wives, sisters, and daughters at home, whereas education for boys and men was far more comprehensive. Such inequality was why, in 1900, she established *Joshi Eigaku Juku* ('Women's Institute for English Studies') in Tokyo to afford women equal opportunities to pursue higher education in the liberal arts. She established the Women's Institute with the help of Alice Bacon[5] and Princess Ōyama, her friend from the Iwakura Mission and the first woman in Japan to earn a college degree. After World War II, the Women's Institute became Tsuda University, now one of the most prestigious institutes of higher education for women in Japan. In 1905, Tsuda also became the first president of the Japanese branch of the World Young Women's Christian Association (YWCA).

Shigeko Nagai

Shigeko Nagai (1861–1928) was a Christian educator, one of the first two women in Japan to attend college, and one of the first piano teachers in the country. In 1871, as part of the Iwakura Mission sent to the United States, Nagai moved into the home of John Stevens Cabot Abbott in New Haven,

---

5   Alice Mabel Bacon (1858–1918) was an American writer, women's educator and a foreign advisor to the Japanese government during the Meiji period.

Connecticut, where she grew up and graduated from New Haven High School. In 1878, she entered the School of Art at Vassar College in Poughkeepsie, New York, where, together with Princess Ōyama (1860–1919), she became the first woman from Japan to enroll in college.

Nagai earned a degree in music from Vassar in 1881, and after returning to Japan, she served at the Tokyo Women's Normal School as a teacher in Western music. Similar to Tsuda, Nagai was an early advocate for equal education for women, one who was inspired by her faith in Christ. Although the preceding paragraphs are limited to discussing only two members of the Iwakura Mission, all five were invested in women's right to education for the rest of their lives.

Education for Women

At the beginning of the Meiji period, women missionaries offered education to women in Japan. According to "Statistics of Missions and Missionary Work in Japan for the Year 1887," 29 girls' schools had borders in 1887, with 1,716 students in 1886 and 2,707 in 1887. In the latter year, there were only 12 boys' schools, however (Patessio 2011, 78), which indicates the relatively high demand for education for women, inspired by women who were Christian missionaries.

As mentioned, Protestant missionary organizations began their work by sending men to Japan, often accompanied by their wives, who played a crucial role in spreading the Gospel. Clara Hepburn (1818–1906), the wife of Dr. J. C. Hepburn (1815–1911), arrived in Japan in 1859 as a member of the Presbyterian Church and by 1863 had established the Hebon (Hepburn) Juku, a Western-style academy for boys and girls.

Mary Kidder (1834–1910), the first single woman of the American Reformed Church who, along with other unmarried women, was sent to Japan by Protestant mission organizations, would take over the Hepburn Juku and transform it into Ferris Jogakuin ('Ferris Seminary'). The Seminary's teaching faculty briefly included the intellectuals and activists Shizuko Wakamatsu (1864–1896),[6]

Toyoju Sasaki (1853–1901),[7] and one of the first Japanese feminists Toshiko Kishida (1863–1901) (Patessio 2011, 73). Although many men serving as missionaries feared unmarried women missionaries, others followed Kidder's path, including Katherine Tristram, who became the headmistress of Bishop Poole Girls' School in Osaka in 1891. Martha J. Cartmell became the first missionary of the Woman's Missionary Society of the Canadian Methodist Church sent to Japan, and Dora Schoonmaker, of the American Methodist Episcopal Mission, opened Joshi Shogakko, which later became Aoyama Jogakuin, one of the most prestigious schools in Tokyo.

In the decades that followed, Emma Ratz Kaufman (1881–1979), another extraordinary woman missionary, also devoted her life and her wealth to enabling women in Japan access and benefit from equal education. A Canadian born in Berlin to a wealthy family, Kaufman belonged to Zion Evangelical Church and, for more than 25 years, served as a secretary on the Tokyo YWCA staff and as a member of Japan's national YWCA committee. Beginning in 1911,

---

6   Shizuko Wakamatsu was a Japanese novelist, translator, and educator.
7   Sasaki Toyoju was the secretary of Japan's Woman's Christian Temperance Union (WCTU).

she spent the next 27 years of her life helping to raise the standing of women in Japan by means of social and religious education. In 1918, Kaufman was appointed deputy secretary of the Tokyo YWCA, a position that she accepted without taking a salary, and she would later donate a considerable portion of her large inheritance to the YWCA in Nagoya and Kyoto. She also sponsored 27 young women from Japan to study abroad and supported 12 others from the United States and Canada to work in Japan.

In relaying those exemplary women's work, it is essential to mention that women missionaries sent to Japan invariably preached and trained women in Japan within the framework of Christian patriarchy:

> Women missionaries told Japanese women that their duty was to become good Christian mothers and wives. However, they also showed them that women's work was as important as men's, that women's dependence on their husbands was not necessarily the rule, and that women could have a rewarding life outside of their homes by working for the good of society while their household chores did not necessarily have to take precedence over more important tasks such as learning. (Patessio 2011, 75-76)

According to Karen Seat (2003, 328), although many Japanese first viewed women mission schools as a cost-effective way to educate women, government officials increasingly criticized the schools and the type of woman that they produced, particularly when their graduates "became active in movements demanding women's rights, especially as participants of the broader Popular Rights movement." Seat thus confirms Rose's finding that, according to the Ministry of Education as well as government-sponsored newspapers, mission schools "had the wrong view of female education" and produced women "who walk like men" (Rose 1992, 50). Nevertheless, during the Meiji period, Christian education for women played a crucial role in women's emancipation and gave birth to feminist movements inspired by Christianity.

Christian Women and Women's Rights

Following the chapter's earlier case study of the Bluestockings as proponents for and in women's movements in Japan, this part of the chapter discusses the Christian influence on such movements. Here, I do not use the word *feminism* in describing the era, because Christian advocacy for women's rights remained patriarchal at the base. Even so, Christianity played a major role in helping women to mobilize and advocate for their rights.

Among the best-known Christian movements for women's rights during the Meiji period was the Woman's Christian Temperance Union (WCTU). The WCTU was initially organized in Hillsboro, Ohio, on December 23, 1873, before becoming officially established in 1874 at a national meeting in Cleveland. A decade later, the World WCTU was founded in 1883 as the organization's international arm; it currently has branches in Australia, Canada, Germany, Finland, India, Japan, New Zealand, Norway, South Korea, Great Britain, and the United States. At its inception in 1874, the WCTU's stated goal was to create a "sober and clean world" through abstinence, chastity, and evangelical Christianity. Its first chairman was Annie Turner Wittenmyer (1827–1900), an American social reformer, humanitarian, and writer and, serving from 1874 to 1879, the first president of the Women's Christian Temperance Association.

The WCTU was founded at a time when Japan, a country on the other side of the world, was an ambitious new nation undergoing modernization that presented an ideal setting for operating the newly established WCTU. Mary Greenleaf Clement Leavitt (1830–1912), the world's first missionary for the WCTU, traveled extensively worldwide, including in Japan, where, as in other countries, she waged a crusade against alcohol and its evils, including domestic violence, and advocated for women's suffrage and equal rights, including the right to higher education. Leavitt arrived in Yokohama on June 1, 1886, where she met Clara and James Curtis Hepburn, Presbyterian missionaries who would arrange lectures for her during her five-month stay in Yokohama, Tokyo, Nikko, Hieizan, Kyoto, Osaka, Wakayama, Sakai, Kobe, Okayama, and Nagasaki. The Hepburns' connections in those cities generally derived from a network of Christian men, all from former samurai families, with local WCTU chapters, save the Tokyo WCTU chapter, which was organized on December 6, 1886, after Leavitt had already left Japan. Throughout her life, Leavitt also published work advocating temperance on the basis of science, much of which was translated into Japanese.

On the whole, the WCTU in Japan has advocated reducing the consumption of alcohol, if not total abstinence from alcoholic beverages, and has been active in several areas of social reform, including the amendment of Japanese concubine laws, pushes for better education and health benefits, and campaigns for women's suffrage. By 1939, the organization had more than 9,100 adult and youth members and 186 branches across Japan (Lublin 2010, 173).

Kajiko Yajima

After attending some of Leavitt's lectures in Tokyo, Kajiko Yajima (1833-1925) and 28 other women were inspired to establish the Tokyo WCTU, with Yajima appointed president and Toyoju Sasaki serving as secretary. For 40 years in and around that time, Yajima was the director of a Presbyterian missionary school for girls in Tokyo and the founder of the Women's Reform Society. An educator, pacifist, and Christian activist, Yajima vigorously supported the cause of education and advocated the elimination of prostitution in Japan, both of which challenged Japan's patriarchal views on women's status in society. She also edited the *Japanese Temperance Journal*, delivered lectures, led protest marches, raised funds, and represented Japan at international conferences.

In their book *Ten Against the Storm*, Mariana Nugent Prichard and Norman Young Prichard (1957, 63–64) write the following about Yajima:

> But it was not only in education that Kaji Yajima served her country's people. Her heart wept for the backward, stammering school girls who came to her classrooms from homes terrorized by drunken fathers. She had never forgotten her own longing for family serenity. Sake, rice wine, was Kaji's lifelong enemy. The little lady decided to make a declaration of war against it . . .
>
> Kaji Yajima's pride was the little village of Kawadami, where the people had needed a 45,000-yen school for their children. The village fathers put their heads together and figured that they had been drinking up 9,000 yen worth of sake every year. They decided

to do without rice wine for five years and put up a school with the money they saved. Even the eight sake dealers joined the enterprise, and the new school appeared on schedule. Other villages caught the enthusiasm of Kawadami . . .

Kaji Yajima felt the time had come for Japan to build strong families through faithful devotion like the love she had seen in her father and mother. When Emperor Meiji's Diet assembled for the first time in 1890, Mrs. Yajima introduced a bill outlawing prostitution and calling for faithfulness "between one man and one woman." To every new Diet after that time Mrs. Yajima brought her "one man, one woman" bill. She received so many threatening letters that she took to wearing a white death robe under her somber matronly kimono.

In 1921, Yajima even appeared before U.S. president Warren G. Harding before a conference on disarmament and addressed him with words inspired by her Christian faith and activism:

Mr. President, as a Christian woman of Japan I have come to America to pray for the success of the coming conference for the limitation of armaments. . . . I perceive the invitation which you sent to the Japanese government is based on the Christian faith, and I wish to see the Christian foundations for the conference reinforced by prayer. (Prichard and Prichard 1957, 67)

Beyond the WCTU and its members, other individual Christian women in Japan contributed to women's emancipation in Meiji Japan. For instance, Princess Ōyama became director of the National Women's Association and Red Cross Nursing Association.

The modernization of Japan during the Meiji era not only opened the way for Christian reintegration and missionary activity but also laid the groundwork for future women's activism, advocacy, emancipation. The following chapter describes the outcomes of what women achieved throughout the Meiji period.

WOMEN & CHRISTIANITY

in Taishō and Early Shōwa Period, 1912-1945

Chapter Three

WOMEN & CHRISTIANITY
in Taishō and Early Shōwa Period, 1912-1945

The death of Emperor Meiji in 1912 marked the end of the Meiji era in Japan, which gave way to the Taishō period (1912–1926), followed by the Shōwa period (1926–1989). This chapter focuses on both the Taishō and Shōwa periods until the end of World War II in 1945. Since the latter period continued after Japan's capitulation to the Allied Forces, the role of Christian women in the postwar period is discussed in Chapter 4.

After Emperor Meiji's death, his son Yoshihito (1879–1926) became the 123rd emperor of Japan. Each time a new emperor ascends to the throne, a new era begins with an appointed name called "Nengō", mostly selected from old Chinese Confucian books; the period of Emperor Yoshihito's reign is called *Taishō* ('great righteousness'), which he announced in his coronation speech. As its name indicates, the Taishō period is generally known as the era for democratization in Japan, in a form called "Taishō democracy." The transformation came about partly due to the new emperor's struggles with health problems, which caused political power to shift from the *genrō* ('elders') to the Imperial Diet of Japan and the democratic parties. Because the military did not initially influence or control the formation of the cabinet, several administrations during the Taishō period operated free from military intervention, especially during 1918–1922 and 1924–1926.

During the Taishō era, Japan established a monarchy inspired by the British parliamentary system, a constitutional democracy with a two-party political structure. As a result, the country grew into a modern state similar to contemporary Western nations. Despite Japan's rapid development and the blossoming of urban life during the period, modernization and industrialization came at the expense of rural communities. As peasants in the countryside and impoverished laborers signaled unrest and organized many demonstrations and strikes in response, socialism and communism began to spread rapidly among the Japanese population, in opposition to established conservative and nationalistic ideas that were predominantly patriarchal.

In parallel, another stream of thought active in Japanese society at the time was Christianity. The missionary work during the Meiji period, sparked by the reentry of Christianity in Japan, began to bear fruit in the form of rising numbers of foreign and native Christians in the country. Both men and women in those groups increasingly contributed to Japanese society not only at theological and intellectual levels but also in movements for social justice. This chapter aims to describe the role of Christian women in Japan in both the religious and societal realms, first by briefly characterizing the general condition of the women's rights movement in the island nation.

Women Rights in the Taishō and Early Shōwa Periods

The foundation of the women's rights movement in Japan had been laid during the Meiji period when education played a vital role in the movement's inception. Although Meiji authorities restricted women's education to the service of the patriarchal family system, women did not cease their struggle for equal education for both genders.

During the Taishō period, the women's rights movement began addressing women's suffrage in Japan. Japanese law prohibited women from participating in politics, expressing political views, and participating in political demonstrations. In 1920, however, participation in politics became a priority for women, and in 1921, the National Assembly allowed women to participate in political demonstrations under the Police Security Act. In 1922, owing to feminists such as Fusae Ichikawa (1893–1981) and Raichō Hiratsuka (1886–1971), women could engage in Japan's political processes, which encouraged them to organize political meetings. When a violent earthquake struck Tokyo the following year, delegates from 43 organizations joined the Tokyo Federation of Women's Organizations (Tokyo Rengo Fujinkai). Even though the Federation chiefly aimed to aid victims of the earthquake, it became one of the most prominent women's activist movements of its time. The Federation organized itself around five major domains—governmental, social, educational, employment, and labor—and within each, women actively organized themselves into a corresponding group to address problems in Japanese society.

Thanks to the government group of the Federation, the Women's Suffrage League (Fusen Kakutoku Domei), was born and soon became the most significant, opinionated women's advocacy movement of the era. Above all, the League demanded the political right for women to achieve public recognition at the national and local levels of government. The League's manifesto, issued to address the abuses that women in Japan had suffered for centuries, argued that such suffering would cease if centuries-long customs in Japan were abolished and a new Japan has constructed that recognized natural rights for both men and women. The manifesto also emphasized the injustice of excluding women from universal suffrage, for women had become educated during the previous 50 years of the Meiji period, and stressed the importance of uniting women of different religions and occupations in a movement for women's suffrage. Last, it demanded political rights for the protection of working women and women laboring in their own households. However, the public and political response characterized the League's members as being selfish in ignoring their duties at home and striving to be publicly active in politics, which was considered to be the work of men.

Women and Christianity

Despite all of the prejudices and limitations that existed in Japanese society for women, women in Japan came to be highly involved in political and economic processes in Japan in the early decades of the 20th century. In various areas both within the Church and in society, Christian women in Japan were especially active. They played the critical role of advocates in movements for labor and social justice, consumer rights, reproductive rights, and suffrage within international organizations of Christians, including the Young Women's Christian Association (YWCA) and the Woman's Christian Temperance Union (WCTU).

Asako Hirooka (1849–1919), a prominent Christian woman during the Taishō period, was born during the Meiji period and converted to Christianity in 1911. Before her conversion, Hirooka was regarded as one of Japan's first businesswomen, one who was involved in the coal mining, banking, and even life insurance industries. Under the influence of Jinzo Naruse (1858–1919), Hirooka was baptized in 1911 by Rev. Tsuneteru Miyagawa (1857–1936), a pioneer of the Osaka YMCA, and became an enthusiastic Christian as a member of the Japanese YWCA and involved herself in religious activities as well. After becoming Christian, she was often invited as a keynote speaker at Christian events and ranked among the leaders of the 1912 YWCA Summer Conference. As a close friend of Eiichi Shibusawa (1840–1931), Tsuda, Merel Voliz, and Princess Ōyama, she was also active in social work and service, including in abolitionist and women's movements. Hirooka asked Japanese society, "Why do you hold it against the women who sell their bodies? Because they do not have any other choice. So, what is the story? Because men deny them the right to educate their daughters."[1] With her numerous editorials published in women's magazines one after the other, she strove to educate women in Japan about their rights. With her wealth, knowledge, leadership skills, and passion for women's education, she ultimately helped to establish Japan's Women University.

---

1   https://jpreki.com/hirookaasako/

In 1934, Christian activists Michi Kawai (1877–1953) and Ochimi Kubushiro (1882–1972) published a remarkable book, *Japanese Women Speak: A Message from the Christian Women of Japan to the Christian Women of America,* that provided an extensive account of Christian women's influence in Japan up until that time. In their book, Kawai and Kubushiro described how Christian women in Japan had been prominent in various areas, including educational work, religious mission work, and work in the church, and, as such, had expanded charity work, significantly impacted family life, and contributed to international peace, all of which had helped to build the new Japan.

Both Kawai and Kubushiro played vital roles in Christianity in Japan. Kawai, an educator, Christian activist, and the first Japanese national secretary of the YWCA, had been a student of Tsuda. In 1929, she also became the founder of a school for young women, Keisen Jogaku-en, whose first class contained nine students. As enrollment grew as the years passed, the school eventually gave birth to Keisen University, founded in 1988 in Tama, Tokyo.

By comparison, Kubushiro, the daughter of Christian clergyman Kubo Shinjirō, became prominent in activism for the abolition of prostitution in Japan. In 1916, she joined Fujin Kyofukai, the Japanese branch of the U.S. WCTU, run by her grandaunt, Kajiko Yajima. As a member of the Women's Suffrage League, Fujin Kyofukai was one of the primary organizers of the First Congress of Women of All Japan in 1930. In 1971, Kubushiro became Honorary Chairman of the Japanese WCTU, and she was later awarded the Medal of Honor of the Blue Ribbon and the Third Class of Merit of the Order of the Sacred Treasure. Kubushiro's publications include *The Life of Kajiko Yajima* and *The Path to the Abolition of Prostitution: An Autobiography.*

Evangelism, Missions, and Church Work

Along with Kubushiro, Kawai wrote, "Indeed there are many Dorcases, Lydias and Priscillas whose courage, loyalty and sacrifices have enriched and are enriching the Japanese church" (Kawai and Kubushiro 1934, 6–7). Kawai and Kubushiro argued that thanks to qualified Bible schools and women's theological seminaries with high academic standards, Christian women in Japan, more than ever before, were involved in individual evangelism and evangelism in the public sphere. During rice-planting seasons, they offered daily services at Bible schools as well as free kindergartens and day nurseries for peasant families who had to spend their days performing agricultural labor (Kawai and Kubushiro 1934, 7).

According to Kawai and Kubushiro (1934,4), the term 'evangelism' was not limited to big meetings in Japan. Women were involved in a variety of forms of evangelization. This category encompasses a wide variety of meetings in homes, churches, schools, theaters, boats, and shops where the Gospel of Jesus Christ was shared with non-Christians. Kawai and Kobushiro's book mentions some prominent women missionaries and evangelists in Japan during the prewar period, including Hatsune Hasegawa (Kobe Congregational Church), Tomi Furuta (Methodist), Tamaki Kawado Uemura (Christ's Church in Japan), Kiku Ishihara (Baptist), Kinu Sekiya (Episcopal), Koto Yonemura (Lutheran), and Toku Hirase (Evangelical).

Women not only evangelized on their own but also organized themselves into evangelistic and missionary associations. Kawai and Kubushiro describe how various Christian women's societies united to spread the Gospel in Japan and even among the Japanese diaspora.[2] Although those women's mission societies had European and American roots, in 1933 they were all presided over by native Japanese women. For example, the *Yearbook of the Japanese Women's Conferences of the Methodist Episcopal Church* for 1928 reports that at its general conference in fall 1927, the Japanese Methodist Church legally recognized the Society of Sisters as a separate body of women, one with the aim of supporting evangelism and, in turn, the Japanese Methodist Church in general. Kawai and Kubushiro (1934, 10) wrote that some women of the Methodist Church are "doubtless doing social work at the same time, but that one and all take the responsibility for some direct evangelistic work goes without saying. This Church leads in Christian social service, such as settlement work, care for the blind and orphans, day nurseries, kindergartens for every social class, night schools, etc. These trained women work in the double capacity of teacher and evangelist."

In 1932, Furuta was selected as superintendent of the Woman's Work Department of the Methodist Church. Furuta was a remarkable speaker who, according to Kawai

---

2   Congregational Women's Mission Society (est. 1906) of Kobe
    Congregational Church, Methodist Women's Work Department (est.
    1931), Women's Mission's Society of the Church Christ (est. 1913) of
    the Presbyterian and Reformed Churches, Baptist Women's
    Department (est. 1933), Japanese Praying Women, the Fujin Kai of the
    United Lutheran Church, and the Evangelical Women's Mission
    Society (est. 1918).

and Kubushiro, could bring the direct message of the Gospel to any audience. Furuta's conviction, passion, and sincerity never failed, and she ranked among the primary speakers at both Christian conferences and girls' and women's meetings. She was also active in social work for Christians (Kawai and Kubushiro 1934, 11).

In October 1930, Tamaki Kawado Uemura (1890–1982), the third daughter of one of Japan's famous early Protestant church leaders and theologians, Masahisa Uemura (1858–1925), began to evangelize at her home in Yodobashi, Tokyo. The following year, she founded the Kashiwagi Mission Church, and in 1934, in the Tokyo Chukai of the Japanese Christian Church, Uemura became Japan's second ordained woman pastor. In 1937, she founded the Japanese YWCA as it is known today and began serving as president. After serving as vice president of the World YWCA from 1938 to 1951, she was named Honorary Chairman of the Japanese YWCA. As vice president, on April 30, 1946, she was the first civilian to travel to the United States to convey a message from Japan to President Harry S. Truman. Upon returning to Japan, she gave a weekly lecture on the Bible to the three Imperial Daughters and subsequently to the Empress Nagako herself for four years until 1951. She also rebuilt the Kashiwagi Church, which had burned down in 1947.[3] Uemura was delighted by pioneering evangelism and passionate about sharing the Gospel. Her sermons were powerful, and with a prophetic emphasis on suffering and mourning with those who weep.

---

3 https://www.wellesley.edu/ealc/alum-corner/japan-alum/
    tamaki-uemura-1915-

Kawai and Kubushiro's (1934,16) book indicates that 10 well-known Christian training schools and 327 Christian kindergartens with 16,580 children were operating in Japan in 1931. However, because those schools had been supervised and supported by different mission boards, which felt that the time had come for leadership to be transferred to the people of Japan, the Baptist mission transferred authority over their training school to Kiku Ishihara (1884–1967). Ishihara, born in Chōfu, Yamaguchi Prefecture, had graduated from Shoei Nursery and Welfare College before traveling to the United States in 1905, where she obtained qualification as a kindergarten teacher from the University of Cincinnati before returning to Japan. In 1917, upon returning to the United States, she studied at Columbia University's Faculty of Education before again returning to Japan with an M.A. degree. A pioneer of kindergartens in Japan that offered progressive childcare as in the West, she also served as the chairperson of the Christian Childcare Federation in Kanto and conducted a series of educational tours throughout the United States after the war. In 1963, Ishihara received a doctorate from Weston University in the U.S. state of Florida. Although more of a missionary and educator than an evangelist, she did practice evangelism through missions.

Similar to Ishihara, Kinu Sekiya, a devoted member of the Episcopal Church and wife of the vice minister of the Imperial House, was more of a missionary than an evangelist. A supporter of the needy and suffering, especially lepers, she contributed financially to the work of Kusatsu Leper Hospital (Kawai and Kubushiro 1934, 18).

Another evangelist-cum-missionary during the prewar period was Koto Yonemura of the Lutheran Praying Women, Fujin Kai. Kawai and Kubushiro (1934, 20) wrote the following about Fujin Kai and the Lutheran missions in Japan:

> It must be remembered that the membership of the entire Lutheran Church of Japan was not over 3,500 and that there were only nineteen women's societies at that time. But that number included women of ability, consecration, and a broadening vision. So that, even at the first convention, which was held at Kumamoto in the Spring of 1928, it was apparent that Japanese Lutheran women were ready to fall in line with the thousands of women of other countries to work for the bringing in of Christ's Kingdom on earth.

In that context, Yonemura, a passionate evangelist, and speaker who placed prayer at the center of her calling to God was chosen as the leader of the convention. Kawai and Kubushiro (1934, 20) described her as a woman of unusual consecration and openness to the service of Christ.

Toku Hirase of the Evangelical Women's Mission Society was a unique young evangelist who used miniature street theater to tell Bible stories and thus reach out to Japanese children and youth. Inspired by Ōmori,[4] a Christian man who used the paper theater for evangelism in Numazu near Mount Fuji, Hirase developed her own form of miniature street

---

4 Ōmori's first name is unknown.

theater for evangelical work in Fukagawa, a crowded ward of downtown Tokyo. Although her street theater was initially ridiculed for failing to interest children in Bible stories, her perseverance and patience persuaded the children to gather around her and listen to the stories that once they refused to hear. Kawai and Kubushiro (1934, 25) wrote that she "seeks to transform lives, not through social work first, but through personal evangelism."

Mission and Charity

Christian women in Japan during the Taishō period and the first part of the Shōwa period combined evangelism and mission work with charity work and education. One such activity involved outreach among racial minorities such as the Ainu people in Hokkaido and the *burakumin*, a class of outcasts. Even though the Meiji reformation banned the class system as well as discrimination against the *burakumin*, the group was nevertheless discriminated against by the public for several generations to follow. Kawai and Kubushiro (1934) documented in their book that Michiko Miyasaki rescued a girl from among the outcasts and brought her to the Women's Home of the WCTU in Tokyo. Ultimately, becoming convinced that outcasts could find salvation only in Christianity, Miyasaki returned to where they lived and operated her mission among them. To pay her mortgage, she earned income by selling various products, although she dedicated most of her time to working with children and their families (Kawai and Kubushiro 1934, 48).

The upper class of Japanese society was also included in the vision of Christian women in Japan. In their book, Kawai and Kubshiro (1934, 48-49) praised Yuka Noguchi of the Futaba kindergarten, who devoted her life to caring for the children of the social elite and, as such, seized the opportunity to share the Gospel with the parents and to raise funds for the construction of houses to accommodate a day nursery for the poor:

> In the center of this nursery, she had a chapel built and to this chapel, she called together her former pupils, the daughters, and wives of the best families in the nation. And here these women who rather avoided attending Christian churches could come and gather around their teacher, and every time they gathered, they received Christian teaching as well as enthusiasm for social work among the poorer classes of people.

Mission and charity work by women also occurred among the sick. Yae Ibuka (1897–1989), a Roman Catholic Japanese nurse, cared for Japan's population of lepers and, in the process, shared the love of Christ with individuals who were suffering. After her skin disease was misdiagnosed as leprosy and she was hospitalized, she was inspired to help patients who had the disease, and in 1923, she became the only qualified nurse at Koyama Fukusei Hospital, where she was initially admitted for diagnosis. From 1923 until 1978, Ibuka remained the chief nurse at the hospital, where her devotion to patients with leprosy was highly valued, and she later became the Japan Catholic Nurses Association's first president. For her efforts, Pope John XXIII bestowed the Order of St. Sylvester upon her in 1959. Kinu Sekiya, the wife of the vice minister of the Imperial House in 1933, was a devout Christian who also supported work to help lepers, as did many other Christian women from various backgrounds and social classes.

Along with being active in nursing, Christian women in Japan also became doctors, and some even founded medical colleges as part of their mission work. After many challenges, one of them, Yayoi Yoshioka (1871–1959), became a physician and in 1900 started a medical college, Tokyo Women's Medical School, with only one student, Shigeyo Takeuchi (1881–1975), who was also baptized and trained by Masahisa Uemura. For women, the institution was vital as a sole place in Japan until 1930 where women could study medicine, due to their being denied that right at imperial and private universities. Yoshioka was the 27th woman to receive her medical license in Japan after the Meiji period and was also active in the women's suffrage movement. Added to her, the first woman doctor to obtain a degree in Western medicine in Japan was Ginko Ogino (1851–1913), who, in 1890, married Yukiyoshi Shikata, a Protestant clergyman and utopian visionary, and moved to Hokkaido with him in 1894, where she ran a medical practice. After he died in 1908, she returned to Tokyo, resumed running a hospital, and would also participate in the WCTU.

Christian women in Japan were also active among women factory workers. In the 1930s, according to Kawai and Kubushiro (1934), approximately 1,004,000 women worked in factories engaged in silkworm cultivation, silk spinning, and the manufacture of cotton goods. Viewing the sheer number of women factory workers as an opportunity for mission work among women, Christian missions sent missionaries to various factories on Sundays or weekdays, whenever it was possible, to conduct religious meetings among the workers there (Kawai and Kubushiro 1934, 54–55).

One of the most significant contributions made by Christian women in Japan was the provision of support to prostitutes and the establishment of shelters for their abandoned or so-called "illegal" children. To be sure, prostitution was licensed and thriving in Japan during the era. According to Manako Ogawa (2004, 102), of the 586 pleasure districts recorded nationwide in 1881, 243 (41%) had received government approval following the Meiji Restoration in 1868. Enticed by false promises made by pimps or sold by their parents to save their families from poverty, thousands upon thousands of poor women in Japan were licensed as prostitutes, locked up in certain districts of cities, and not permitted to leave without permission, such that they were often referred to as *kago no naka no tori* ('caged birds'). Beyond that, brothel owners frequently took advantage of the prostitutes' lack of education (Ogawa 2004, 116). In response, at the beginning of the 20th century, Kieko Yamamuro (1874–1916) opened her home to shelter prostitutes who had escaped the threat of brothel keepers. The wife of Brigadier General Gunpei Yamamuro (1874–1940) and the first head of the Salvation Army in Japan, Yamamuro was a Christian social worker who helped and advocated for prostitutes and women at risk of prostitution. Masahisa Uemura baptized her as well. In 1916, while hosting a benefit event to raise funds for a tuberculosis sanatorium, Yamamuro collapsed and died, and the following year, Kieko Memorial Hall was built in the Salvation Army Sanatorium in her honor.

The sacrifices presented above are only a few of the ones made by Christian women before World War II, who collectively offered charity to the poor, the oppressed, and the marginalized. During the 1920s, as they continued to advocate for women's rights in Japan, Christian women in Japan and other feminist movements also condemned growing domestic repression, the spread of war in Asia, and Japanese foreign policy.

Wartime

By the end of the 1930s, Christian women in Japan had abandoned their efforts in social causes due to persecution and imprisonment by the national government. The Japanese WCTU, for instance, had no choice but to cut ties with the World WCTU, and in 1941, with the outbreak of the Pacific War, the WCTU and other Christian organizations in Japan redirected their transnational efforts toward Asia. Under Japan's military regime, the Japanese WCTU had few options to function in China as well. Although they offered charity such as medical services to women in China, the effort was mostly organized as propaganda by the government to create a positive image of the Japanese Empire.

Even though Christian women in Japan remained active in education and social work prior to the war and attempted to act as loyal citizens of a government that was becoming increasingly militaristic, growing tensions between Japan and the West harmed the image of Christianity in Japan. Throughout the war itself, Japanese Christian women organizations likewise struggled to maintain their Christian perspective. While their activities were suppressed and self-censured on the surface, Japanese Christian women organizations actively sought to minimize their activities that supported the Japanese government. Because most missionaries had left Japan before the Pacific War and because the native Christians who remained were treated with suspicion, they suffered just as much as the rest of the population, if not more, during the war.

Far more remains to be written about Christian women's work in Japan during the Taishō period and the years before World War II ended. Many of those women, as well as their deeds of love and sacrifice for the benefit of the Gospel and the development of women's status in society, deserve to be acknowledged despite going unmentioned in the preceding paragraphs. Nevertheless, I hope that this chapter has provided an overview of the valuable work that Christian women in Japan contributed to the Church and society at large during the era.

WOMEN & CHRISTIANITY

in Postwar and Contemporary Japan

Chapter Four

WOMEN & CHRISTIANITY
in Postwar and Contemporary Japan

The term *postwar Japan* refers to the era following Japan's surrender to the Allied Forces in 1945 until today. In Japan, the era can be divided into three distinct periods—the late Shōwa period (1945–1989), the Heisei period (1989–2019), and the Reiwa period (2019–present)—each linked to the reign of a specific emperor. During the late Shōwa period, Emperor Hirohito reigned over Japan, while Emperor Akihito reigned during the Heisei period, and Emperor Naruhito currently reigns during the Reiwa period.

From 1945 into the 21st century, Japanese society and culture have undergone rapid change, as has the role of women in society. As a result, describing the shifting status, role, and place of women in Japanese society during the past eight decades in a single chapter is quite a challenge. To provide scope, most of this chapter is devoted to Christian women in Japan from 1945 to the present. Above all, it seeks to clarify what Christian women in Japan have accomplished thus far, what they have contributed to Christianity in modern Japan, and what their challenges are today.

Postwar Japan

The Pacific War and the establishment of the U.S.-led occupation of Japan brought about the end of state Shintoism in the country as well as emperor worship. After the war, missionaries retook the stage in Japan in 1945, following the restoration of religious freedom and the separation of church and state as guaranteed by Japan's postwar constitution. Japan's growing power and the atrocities committed by the Japanese military during World War II, together with the attack on Pearl Harbor, gave U.S. forces justification to attack Hiroshima and Nagasaki with atomic bombs. Those weapons of mass destruction, invented by the United States, were used for the first time in Japan, which effectively ended the war in 1945 and resulted in Japan's surrender on August 14, 1945.

Just days prior, on August 9, 1945, the second of two atomic bombs—the only two ever used as instruments of aggression against essentially defenseless civilian populations—was dropped on Nagasaki in an attack that devastated the oldest center of Christianity in the country (Kohls, 2007). As Kohls (2007) has noted, not only was Nagasaki the site of the largest Christian church in the East, St. Mary's Cathedral, but it also had the largest concentration of baptized Christians in all of Japan. Seat (2003, 333-334) has added that in 1945, the U.S. firebombing of approximately 60 Japanese cities destroyed numerous mission schools and other mission-related structures. Both Hiroshima and Nagasaki had Methodist girls' schools, and the atomic bomb destroyed Hiroshima Jogakkō, killing 350 students, faculty, and staff. Numerous students of Kwassui Girls' School in Nagasaki also perished. On August 15, 1945, a day after Japan's capitulation to the Allied Forces, Emperor Hirohito announced Japan's unconditional surrender in a nationwide radio broadcast.

By the end of World War II, Japan was a nation exhausted both physically and morally, as historian John W. Hall (1991) has noted. According to Hall (1991, 349), since the outbreak of the Second Sino–Japanese War in 1937, 3.1 million Japanese, including 800,000 civilians, had lost their lives, and more than 30% of the Japanese population had lost their homes. With barely functional transportation systems, acute food shortages spread that reduced much of the country to near-starvation. As farmers reaped tremendous profits by selling food on the black market, civilian morality eroded, and wealthy families were known to barter heirlooms for the necessities of life (Hall 1991, 350). The nation's industry had been crippled to one-quarter of its previous capacity, and the country's economy was on the verge of massive inflation. After being fed exaggerated wartime propaganda and hyper-nationalist values year after year, all of which lost force with Japan's unconditional surrender, the people of Japan were also emotionally and intellectually bewildered (Hall 1991, 350).

Women in Postwar and Contemporary Japan

In 1945, Japan was an occupied, conquered, and defeated superpower, a fallen imperialist nation. All that remained of the country were the ruins of war and it was plagued by chaos, poverty, and disease. Amid such despair, women in Japan began to reposition themselves in Japan's social, cultural, and political scenario, and new hope for their status was kindled with the granting of universal suffrage to women in Japan. After a constitution similar to the U.S. Constitution was implemented and Japan's democratic system restored, women were finally granted the right to vote. On April 10, 1946, 67% of the approximately 20 million women who were eligible to vote did so, and 79 women candidates ran for seats, 39 of whom were elected (Fujiwara-Fanselow and Kameda 1995, 1). Thus, hope that women's right to vote and the recent elections would translate into social and economic equality flourished (Faison 2017).

Ratified in 1946, Japan's new constitution required establishing a judiciary and legislative council to discuss the revision of the Civil Code, especially as it concerned the prewar family system, called *ie*. Natsu Kawasaki (1889–1966), a council member at the time, reported receiving nearly 63,000 letters from women expressing their dissatisfaction with their lives. Some women suffered due to economic turmoil, others suffered due to family strife, and the conclusion was that all of those problems were rooted in the *ie* system. Kawasaki argued that if the prewar family system were revised, then women would raise joyful voices, and she urged council members to listen to those voices. As a result, when the Civil Code was altered and reissued in 1947, women were no longer barred from participating in the *ie* system (Fujiwara-Fanselow and Kameda 1995, 11).

Although *ie* is the indigenous term for the *family* in Japan, it does not convey the same meaning of the word family as used in the West. *Ie* can be translated as 'house' or 'building' but is used in a broader sense to mean 'family' or 'kin.' As a hierarchical family system founded on Confucian principles of honor and loyalty, *ie* governed all relationships within the entire family structure, consisting of the primary family and various subfamilies under it (Lee 2015, 27). According to Reischauer and Graig (1989), the premodern, prewar Japanese family, as part of the *ie* system, could include a subordinate branch of the family, one under the authority of the primary family, and other members who were distant relatives or not related. Such families, with the father or family council exercising absolute authority over individual members, thrived among more prominent members of the feudal warrior class, wealthy merchants, and certain peasant groups (Reischauer and Graig, 1989). In that kin network, relationships between the elderly and the young were based on loyalty and indebtedness and were oriented toward duty, which the system's members considered to be paramount. In turn, the duty-based system influenced how men and women interacted and gave men far higher status than women, who were expected to meet their husbands' every need. As a result, marriages were arranged in the *ie* system based on social status and the women's suitability to fulfill her husband's *ie* obligations. Love between a husband and wife was not considered to be necessary, and lovelessness was not considered to impair a couple's obligation to one another or to the *ie* system (Lee 2015, 28).

In reaction to the system, women started to reorganize themselves into leftist socialist, liberal, and religious groups ignited by the hope of reforming women's status in Japanese society. Among them, Raichō Hiratsuka (1886–1971) organized an international women's rally, the Mothers' Conference, which comprised mothers from around the world, regardless of ideology, creed, race, and class, to "protect the lives of children from the dangers of nuclear war." More broadly, the new women's movement aimed to promote the interests of women as well as children in the new violent, nuclear age (Maxson 2017). The Mothers' Congress was significant because it separated the concept of motherhood from the wartime era by stressing how the wartime state had hijacked motherhood and how the Mothers' Congress would be a vehicle through which women reclaimed historical agency by liberating mothers from the wartime state's hegemonic construction of motherhood (Maxson 2017).

During the war, women had been cast as mothers, or potential mothers, who needed to obey the state by raising sons into soldiers as a sacrifice for the war effort. However, that misguided view on women and motherhood changed after the war, especially due to women activists in the early postwar years who argued that women were now responsible, along with the government, for rectifying social inequalities. Among them, Hideko Maruoka (1903–1990) believed that women should begin by changing the everyday language used to discuss social and, in turn, spark widespread language reform. To that end, Maruoka insisted that

> Women could start by altering the everyday language that they used to express their place in society. Instead of referring to her husband as "master" *(shujin)*, a woman could call him "husband" *(otto)*. Women could avoid phrases like "take a wife" *(yome wo morau)* and say "marry" *(kekkon suru)* instead. Women could stop merely listening to their husbands' ideas and start thinking for themselves first. Maruoka suggested that women remember to stop treating their daughters differently from their sons and that they create an atmosphere in the home of social equality. (Faison 2017, 40)

From postwar Japan into the early 21st century, women in Japan were still socially and culturally expected to be "good wives and wise mothers." In 1947, a typical Japanese woman could expect to have 4.5 children in her lifetime, whereas by the beginning of the 21st century, that figure fell to 1.3 (Holloway 2010, 3). According to the latest statistics available from the National Institute of Population and Social Security Research, in 2015 the fertility rate was slightly higher, at 1.45, but ranks Japan among the most rapidly aging countries in the world. Among the various interpretations of its low fertility rate, Holloway (2010, 4) has written that, according to demographers, women in Japan now wait longer to marry, which reduces the number of years when they are fertile and married, two prerequisites for having children in a country where only 2% of children are born out of wedlock. Holloway (2010, 5) has also highlighted the economists' view—that people in Japan are concerned about the cost of having children—and suggested that due to fiscal stringency, childcare is scarce and of uneven quality, which has resulted in a low fertility rate.

During Japan's economic growth from the mid-1970s to the mid-1980s, being a housewife was regarded as a full-time profession. The full-time housewife was someone who lived in a middle-class urban area with her husband and was responsible for the private domain, including the house, the children, and other domestic matters, while the husband worked in the public sphere. During Japan's economic boom, in some companies, when a woman employee reached the age of 24 years, she was expected to look for a husband, begin caring for her family, and fulfill her responsibilities as a wife. In some cases, a company's president or chief executive officer would even advise young women to start their own families and assist them in finding suitable husbands.

In the 1970s, women's liberation in Japan challenged the role of women in society from a socialist perspective. Proponents of such liberation emphasized how postwar women were trapped in a cycle in which they worked as employees, quit their job upon marriage in their mid-20s and became housewife–mothers, returned to work part-time once child-rearing duties became lighter, and then again quit their jobs to devote themselves to the care of elderly in-laws and aging husbands (Muto 1997, 152). They argued that the cycle was ingrained in Japanese society and culture and imposed, controlled, and maintained through social pressure (Muto 1997, 152). Women's liberationists in 1970s Japan, focusing on so-called "sex liberation," maintained that due to women's reproductive roles, feminists have to rethink procreation and sex. Convinced that preserving the traditional *ie* system would stifle women's sexual desires and result in their oppression, they opposed anti-abortion laws and pushed for the liberalization of the use of contraceptive pills.

According to Women's Lib in Japan,[1] Yumiko Ehara (1952–), Emiko Funamoto, Chizuko Ueno (1948–), and Yayori Matsui (1934–2002) were prominent figures in Japan's Women's Liberation movements. Funamoto's quarterly magazine, *Onna Eros*, has been widely distributed throughout Japan, while Ueno, a sociology professor and author of numerous books on women and family issues, participated in the 1995 World Women's Conference in Beijing. Ehara, for her part, is

---

1   Women's Lib in Japan: http://femjapan.pbworks.com/w/page/8848023/
    Women's%20Lib%20in%20Japan#DeclarationoftheLiberationofEros

a Japanese feminist theorist who has influenced the ideologies and theories behind the women's liberation movement. Last, Matsui was a journalist and co-founder of the Women's International War Crimes Tribunal, which found the entire Japanese government, including Emperor Hirohito, guilty of crimes against comfort women during World War II. She died on December 27, 2002.[2]

Now, just as between 1970 and 2000, attitudes toward traditional gender roles are widely regarded as a significant barrier to achieving gender equality in Japanese society. Ogasawara (2019, 85) indicates that in various surveys, a higher proportion of respondents agreed with the statement, "A man's job is to earn money, and a woman's job is to look after the home and family." According to Ogasawara, some researchers have argued that supporters of traditional gender roles are not necessarily opposed to gender equality but concur with the belief that men and women are equal, as is their work. Such supporters, when women, believe in exercising their role as so-called "maternal gatekeepers" by refusing to surrender their traditional sphere of influence. That theory asserts that although mothers desire fathers to participate in childcare and to support them, they often do not want to relinquish the sense of control that comes with being the primary caregiver of children (Ogasawara 2019, 85).

Until the mid-1980s, full-time housewives in Japan received government tax breaks and were exempted from paying life insurance premiums. However, because of Japan's economic instability and financial crises in the late 1980s and early 1990s, those benefits gradually shifted. In 1985, the Japanese

---

2 Women's Lib in Japan

government developed programs such as the Employment Opportunity Act for Men and Women to encourage housewives to participate in Japan's workforce, which at the time was suffering from a labor shortage. At the end of the 1990s, the passage of the Basic Act for Gender Equal Society encouraged a society in which equality was promoted regardless sex, gender, and age, including in the workforce. In 2015, the Act on Promotion of Women's Participation and Advancement in the Workplace encouraged even more women to contribute to the Japanese economy, which again was suffering from a severe labor shortage. Due to such developments, increasingly more women, both housewives, and single women, chose to take full-time or part-time work, and as a result, the nation's fertility rate dropped.

Though such laws ban gender discrimination and proclaim equal rights for men and women, they do not necessarily affect real-life situations. Gender inequality is indeed visible in educational attainment and the labor market in Japan, and at the 2021 World Economic Forum's Global Gender Gap Report, Japan ranked 120th out of 156 countries in terms of equal rights.[3] Tradition and discrimination contribute to those trends, with evidence showing that women's chances for advancement are poor and that many women work below their potential, and hence prefer to stay at home.

Although increasingly more women in Japan work outside the home, many continue to underachieve professionally. Most women earn less than their male counterparts, and it is rather difficult for women to attain positions of power in

---

3   Global Gender Gap Report 2021, World Economic Forum http:// www.weforum.org/reports/global-gender-gap-report-2021

organizations. In 2021, for example, women occupied only 0.1% of board member positions in Japan's top companies.[4]

At the same time, Japan's economic difficulties are forcing mothers into the workplace, and many Japanese husbands today want their wives to work full-time in order to aid with household expenses. According to Hirata and Warschauer (2014), having a career and a family might seem to make a woman's life more financially secure and emotionally satisfying, but such is not necessarily the case. Hirata and Warschauer (2014, 124) have reported that working women in Japan remain burdened with a disproportionately large share of the housework and childcare, which makes their lives as mothers even harder.

Matahara and *Sekuhara*

Companies in Japan generally disagree that women should try to balance their careers and family lives. Thus, 70% of working women quit their jobs upon having their first child, and some take part-time jobs once their children are in school or grown-up (Hirata and Warschauer 2014, 42). Those women thus quit their jobs in their late 20s or 30s and rejoin the workforce once their children are older, with their participation peaking from 45 to 49 years of age (Hirata and Warschauer 2014, 77). In that way, housework remains the domain of wives in Japan. For most families, a housekeeper is too expensive, and with salarymen husbands working late evenings, wives are the only ones left to clean up. Mothers thus spend most of their time on childcare, cooking, and cleaning (Hirata and Warschauer 2014, 77).

---

4   https://www.nippon.com/en/japan-data/h01071/

Due to such trends, *matahara* ('maternal harassment') has been frequently mentioned in the news media in the past few decades. Working women in companies are discouraged from becoming pregnant, and when they do, some become targets of bullying and harassment, and their employers are liable to psychologically manipulate them into having abortions or leaving their jobs. All of those abuses are forms of *matahara*. In response, Sayaka Osakabe, a victim of *matahara*, has advocated for pregnant women and young mothers who face harassment in the workplace.

At the end of the 1990s, Kazue Muta popularized another term to describe women's mistreatment in Japanese society— *sekuhara* ('sexual harassment')—during her supporting role in the Fukuoka trial of 1989, which arguably introduced the Japanese public to the concept of sexual harassment. In 1989, in a Fukuoka district court, a woman filed Japan's first sexual harassment lawsuit, and, in response, after only a decade, the National Diet amended the Equal Employment Opportunity Law to require employers to prevent sexual harassment in the workplace. Muta argued that, despite growing public awareness of such abuse, *sekuhara* will continue to occur until Japan overhauls the underlying systems that perpetuate workplace discrimination against women.

Meanwhile, some conservative politicians considered full-time housewives to be selfish during the economic boom due to the tax breaks and life insurance premiums that they received, including conservative leaders such as former Prime Minister Yoshiro Mori, who criticized women who choose careers over homemaking, calling them not only selfish but also unpatriotic. In 2003, he also stated that the government should not provide pensions to women who have failed to fulfill their civic duty of having children. Conservatives such as Mori have also blamed Western influence for women's "abandonment" of family life in Japan and the country's dismal birthrate (Holloway 2010, 4).

Although women's situation in postwar Japan has improved, including their access to and participation in the labor market and higher education, and despite the efforts of women's rights activists and advocates in the country, the postwar period has continued to harbor a society oriented toward men. Due to gender inequality's profound place in Japanese culture, women are said to have equal rights but not equal opportunities.

Women and Christianity in Postwar and Contemporary Japan

In the 1970s, Christian women were urged by their faith to engage in various forms of social activism, including advocacy for peace and human rights. According to Watanabe (1991, 132), the trend marked the beginning of Christian women's interest in women's liberation and feminist theology as they gained awareness of their social and religious status. It also coincided with the UN Decade for Women (1975–1985), which inspired the Christian Women of Japan and other organizations to raise the banner of "Equality, Development, and Peace" and create a framework for women's grassroots organizations to operate within. The Japanese Woman's Christian Temperance Union (WCTU), the Young Women's Christian Association (YWCA) of Japan, the National Christian Council of the Japan Women's Committee, and the Association of Roman Catholic Women's Groups all served on the Liaison Committee to prepare for the UN Decade for Women in 1975 (Watanabe 1991, 130).

In general, Christian women in postwar Japan have made significant contributions to the church and society at large in various domains, including social concerns, education, the arts and literature, theology, and the church. The following paragraphs recount the work of some courageous women in postwar Japan whose faith in Christ, despite all obstacles, has motivated and empowered them to shine in a patriarchal church and society.

Social Concerns

Watanabe (1991) had described the social involvement of Christian women in Japan as occurring in the fields of peace, nuclear energy, the environment, prostitution, the issue of South Korean residents in Japan, and the Nakaya trial. During Japan's postwar period, the YWCA of Japan took a solid antinuclear stance, guided by their view on nuclear energy as a symbol of a misguided modern civilization that denies the humanity of all life, including that of humanity itself. In 1971, the YWCA Japan sponsored the Pilgrimage to Hiroshima to raise awareness of their cause (Watanabe 1991, 132):

> Participants in this pilgrimage—Christian and non-Christian, Japanese and non-Japanese—have been confronted and enlightened by a number of issues: the realities of nuclear power, the present state of civilization, the recent history of Japan as an aggressor, foreign atomic-bomb victims (hibakusha), human rights, discrimination, and the environment.

Similar to their counterparts in the prewar period, women's organizations in postwar Japan continued to address the ills of prostitution. In 1973, the Japan WCTU urged all churches and organizations affiliated with the National Christian Council of the Japan Women's Committee to campaign to expose and end the sexual exploitation of South Korean women by wealthy men traveling abroad from Japan (Watanabe 1991, 134). As a result, sex tourism decreased. Thirteen years later, in 1986, the House in Emergency of Love and Peace (HELP) was established to commemorate the WCTU's centennial in Japan. Today, Christian women from across Japan support and assist HELP, which provides aid, refuge, legal advice, and various other services to women. The Roman Catholic Task Force for Asia, meanwhile, is dedicated to assisting Asian women and migrant workers (Watanabe 1991, 134).

Christian women organizations also remained involved in humanitarian activities, while Christian women themselves began to hold important positions in various organizations. Immediately after the war, Japan's counterpart of Mother Teresa, Satoko Kitahara (1929–1958), was a brave, heroic young woman later named one of Japan's most influential women of the 20th century. Kitahara's goal was to help people made poor and underprivileged due to the damages caused by the war. In 1950, she met Zenon Żebrowski, a Conventual Franciscan friar, with whom she worked to provide shelter and support for impoverished people and children who lived in Arinomachi in Asakusa, Tokyo. Kitahara's life revolved around her work until she died of tuberculosis in 1958. In January 2015, Pope Francis confirmed that Kitahara had lived a virtuous Christian life, noted that she was a model of heroic virtue, and thus gave her the title of "Venerable."

Haruko Morimoto (1929–) is a Protestant Christian pastor and evangelist known as a mother to Tokyo's homeless. After a difficult childhood, beginning with kidney disease and abuse by her stepmother years later, Morimoto moved to Tokyo in 1968 with her husband and five children, where her husband, at the age of 40, suffered a stroke that rendered him disabled. For six years, she cared for her paralyzed husband and five children while also performing door-to-door sales and attending theological seminary. Once she began ministering to the homeless and the outcasts of Sanya in Tokyo, she would comb the streets every night looking for lost sheep and prodigal sons and provide them with a hot meal, a shower, and new clothes. In 1973, she was ordained as a pastor.[5]

Miki Sawada (1901–1980), the granddaughter of the founder of the Mitsubishi Zaibatsu conglomerate, Yataro Iwasaki (1835–1885), was a social worker for Japanese American orphans after World War II. Sawada sheltered many mixed-race children who had been abandoned and discriminated against due to their mothers' Japanese ancestry and their fathers' American military service. Upon realizing that she could no longer accommodate all of the children in her own home, Sawada sold everything that she owned and used the revenue to establish the Elizabeth Saunders Home in Oiso, Kanagawa, Japan, named after Elizabeth Saunders, the first donor to the orphanage. In 1949–1950, Sawada traveled across the United States to give lectures and solicit donations for the orphanage.

---

5   https://www.citynews.sg/2013/11/19/dialect-church-service-with-haruko-morimoto-mother-to-tokyos-homeless/

Sadako Ogata (1927–2019), a devout Roman Catholic, political scientist, and UN High Commissioner for Refugees, is another shining example of a Christian woman who was engaged with society and the world. Added to her, Sakie Yokota (1936–), a member of the Nakanoshima Christian Church and the Japan Evangelical Christian Association, has worked to bring back North Korean abductees, including her daughter, Megumi. Meanwhile, Satoko Yamaguchi, a young Christian woman who works as a program coordinator at YWCA Japan, is a member of the World-Generation YWCA's Equality Youth Task Force.

The final figure that I would like to spotlight in this section is Nikki Toyama-Szeto (1974–), another Christian woman who has combined theology with social justice. The executive director of Christians for Social Action, Toyama-Szeto has also held leadership roles at International Justice Mission, the Urbana Conference, and Intervarsity Christian Fellowship (IVP). She enjoys working with communities worldwide, whether through scripture, through thoughtful contemplation on leadership, or by igniting the spiritual imagination. Toyama-Szeto also writes for several journals about justice, leadership, gender issues, and racial justice and is a leading voice for the Mission Alliance. *More than Serving Tea* (IVP 2006) is her co-edited collection of essays, stories, and poetry about the intersection of race, gender, and faith for Asian American women. She also edited the *Urbana Onward* series and cowrote *Partnering with the Global Church* (IVP 2012) with Femi Adeleye as well as *The God of Justice: IJM Institute's Global Church Curriculum* (IVP 2015) with various others.[6]

---

6 https://christiansforsocialaction.org/about-us/our-team/
   nikki-toyama-szeto/

Education

In postwar Japan, Christian women in Japan also continued to play an essential role in education. Educational equality between men and women was granted in Japan's new postwar constitution, and, as a result, women could legally enjoy all forms of education in the same way as men. Even so, because the average Japanese person remained entangled in prewar patriarchal ideas of good wives and mothers, whether postwar Japanese society was prepared for the shift remained dubious.

Among postwar Japan's several prominent Christian women educators and scholars, Kazuko Watanabe (1927–2016), a Roman Catholic nun and essay writer, was an educator and honorary president of Notre Dame Seishin University in 1990. She was also the chairman of the Japan Federation of Catholic Schools from 1992 to 2001. Akiko Minato (1932–), whose Christian roots go back five generations, is a member of the Asagao Church, a professor emeritus of Tokyo Christian University, and the former president of Tokyo Woman's Christian University. In 2014, she was appointed as president of Hiroshima Jogakuin University.

Noriko Hama (1952–), a Roman Catholic since childhood, is a well-known Japanese economist. A professor in Doshisha University's Graduate School of Business, she is an expert in international economics, international finance theory, and European economic theory. She served as a temporary member of the Ministry of Finance's Financial System Council in 2012 and has also served on the Financial Services Agency's Financial Council, the National Tax Agency's National Tax

Review Board, and the Industrial Structure Council of the Ministry of Economy, Trade, and Industry's Special Trade Measures Subcommittee. In 2014, she was appointed as a lecturer at the Democratic Party's Osaka Demokura School. She was also a vocal critic of so-called "Abenomics," the economic policies of Prime Minister Shinzo Abe, for "not looking at the individual people who make a living" and being "incompatible with the globalized economy." She has suggested that that the Japanese economy will collapse if it is not abandoned. In 2009, on Japan's Constitution Day, May 3, she questioned the constitutional amendment regarding foreigners' employment in Japan, claiming that there are signs of "patriotic employment" and that "peace is threatened by discrimination and exclusion." "The Peace Constitution is irreplaceable," she has said, quoting her mother's favorite phrase, "Do not go to war."

Arts and Literature

Inspired by their faith, Christian women in postwar Japan have contributed to many art forms, including literature, cinema, manga, and music. Among them, Machiko Hasegawa (1920–1992) was one of Japan's first women manga artists. She often visited the Bible study group of well-known pastor and professor Tadao Yanaihara (1893–1961), also president of the University of Tokyo.[7] *Sazae-san*, Hasegawa's most famous cartoon work, makes indirect allusions related to biblical personalities and stories as a result of Hasegawa's being a devout Christian who read the Bible every day. The work is said to have been placed on Yanaihara's desk

---

7   Yanaihara belonged to the non-church movement of Kanzo Uchimura (1861–1930)

alongside the Bible. In her honor, the Hasegawa Museum of Art opened in 1985, followed by the Machiko Hasegawa Memorial Hall in 2020.

Sumie Tanaka (1908–2000) was a Tokyo-born playwright best known for her long collaboration with and screenplays for Japan's prominent actress, director, Kinuyo Tanaka (1909–1977), and film director Mikio Naruse. One of her many works is Tsuzumi no onna (Adulteress: The Drum of Waves) from 1995, which showcases adultery from a Christian moral perspective. Tanaka is also well-known for her 1956 work The Life of Gracia Hosokawa, which chronicles the tragic story of Gracia Tama Hosokawa. In 1934, she married Chikao Tanaka (1905–1995), a well-known Japanese writer. At the time, she was an instructor at the Catholic Sacred Heart Women's Academy, and years later, in 1951, she and her children were baptized in the Catholic Church. Many scholars have suggested that her baptism influenced her husband to write plays with Catholic themes.[8]

Mayumi Fukuhara is another Christian film producer and director, one who serves on the boards of several Japanese film festivals and has more than 11 years of experience working at the Tokyo International Film Festival. Fukuhara is also the director of the Damah Film Festival in Tokyo, a competitive festival that focuses on short films about spirituality. Even though Fukuhara became a Christian in the 1990s, her grandparents had long been believers by that time. Yoshiro Fukuhara, her grandfather, was a pastor in Hiroshima's Matoba Church in the 1930s, and after the atomic bombing, he pastored the Hiroshima Tōbu Church. Following her

---

8 https://www.benedictinstitute.org/2019/07/beyond-endo/

conversion, Fukuhara led her parents to the Christian faith, and they were both baptized as a result. Despite her hectic schedule in the film industry, she not only attends services at a local church in Tokyo but is also an active member of the church who occasionally leads prayer and devotionals. During my interview with her, she explained how being a woman and a Christian makes it challenging to live and work in a predominantly patriarchal world while adhering to her Christian faith. She also mentioned that her faith in Christ motivates and empowers her to stay active in such a competitive industry.

Kelly Kozumi Shinozawa is a contemporary Christian manga artist. Born in the city of Toyota, Aichi, she graduated from Nagoya Art College with a concentration in visual design. In 1990, she won the Ribbon Manga Grand Award and has pursued a career as a manga author ever since. In 2002, she completed a certificate program in graphic design at NY Parsons, the New School for Design in New York. Shinozawa moved to New York City in 2002 to study graphic design at the Parsons School of Design. After her roommate shared the Gospel with her, she embraced the Christian faith and was baptized at the Japanese American United Church of Manhattan.[9] Soon after, Shinozawa changed her pen name to Kelly Shinozawa in 2008. Her best-known works are *Manga Messiah* and *Manga Metamorphosis* from *The Manga Bible Series*, which has been translated into 21 languages worldwide,[10] and she received the 2010 Albums Primes

---

9 http://manga-ministry.com/en/profile

10 I met Shinozawa on Facebook and have communicated with her several times. I recall the days when she was working on The Manga Bible Series, during which time she posted photos of herself working, drawing, or consulting with colleagues in the process of creating the work.

Manga Grand Award. Shinozawa has stated the following about her work and mission:

> There are many evangelistic songs and movies but very few Christian mangas. I believe God has given me a mission to communicate His love with the children of the world through manga works. There is joy in drawing and it's fun to make manga, and I'm looking forward to introducing this art medium.[11]

Japan is known throughout the world for its literature, including by Christian novelists such as Shūsaku Endo (1923–1996), author of the renowned novel *Silence* (1966). Not only Endo but also several Christian women in Japan have made significant contributions to Japanese literature, and themes relating to spirituality, morality, and faith can be directly or indirectly traced in their work. A noteworthy example is Ayako Miura (1922–1999), a well-known Christian author during the postwar period whose stories are influenced by biblical themes such as human greed, selfishness, redemption, and sacrifice. After World War II, she was afflicted with severe tuberculosis and subsequently bedridden for several years, which, coupled with her wartime experience, drove her to pessimism and nihilism. However, in 1952, she decided to follow Christ and was baptized in the Protestant church. Many of her works after her new life began as a novelist have become bestsellers, and several have been adapted into feature-length films. One of her most famous novels is *Hosokawa Garasha Fujin* (Shufunotomosha, 1975), translated into English as *Lady Gracia* in 2004.

---

11 http://manga-ministry.com/en/profile

Sawako Ariyoshi (1931–1984) was another well-known writer in postwar Japan, one whose publications address critical social topics such as environmental issues, the challenges faced by older adults in society, and the situation of women in postwar Japan due to the country's pre- and post-war modernization. According to *The Japan Times*, her 1966 work *The Doctor's Wife* is one of the finest examples of Japanese literature from the postwar period. A historical novel, *The Doctor's Wife* dramatizes the roles of women in 19th-century Japan and follows the life of Kae, the wife of Seishū Hanaoka (1760–1835), a pioneering doctor in Japan.[12]

Tomie Ōhara (1912–2000) is another well-known Christian novelist, one who was baptized in a Catholic church at a Tokyo monastery in 1976. The museum dedicated to her, the Ōhara Tomie Museum of Literature, opened in 1991 in her birthplace, the town of Motoyama. Added to her, is Takako Takahashi (1932–2013). Takahashi studied French literature at Kyoto University beginning in 1958, and married award-winning writer Kazumi Takahashi (1931–1971). Despite those successes, Takahashi's life was full of challenges. For one, she had to care for her husband due to his illness, who suffered from colon cancer and eventually passed away in 1971, and after that, she cared for her ill mother as well. Takahashi became a Roman Catholic in 1975. Despite having to overcome numerous obstacles, she continued producing prolifically and received several awards for her works: the Tamura Toshiko Literary Award in 1972 for *To the End of the Sky*, the Women's Literature Award in 1977 for her short stories collection *Lonely Woman*, the Yomiuri Prize in 1985 for her work *Child of Rage*, and the Mainichi Art Award in

---

12 https://en.wikipedia.org/wiki/Sawako_Ariyoshi

2003 for her book Pretty Person. Takahashi became a Roman Catholic nun in 1985 after moving to France.

Hanako Muraoka (1893–1968) was a Japanese Methodist who wrote and translated children's stories. Loretta Leonard Shaw, a Canadian Methodist missionary in Japan from 1905 to 1939, influenced Muraoka by presenting her with the novel *Anne of Green Gables*, which she translated into Japanese during the prewar period. Following the war, the translation became a bestseller and was even included in school curricula in 1970.[13]

It would be amiss to not also mention Ayako Sono (1931–), one Japan's well-known authors of Christian background who was awarded the Pro Ecclesia et Pontifice in 1979.[14] Sono is known for her right-wing conservative views,[15] including her opposition to the matahara movement, and argues that women have no right to work after giving birth and should resign from their employment when pregnant.[16] Furthermore, she favors the racial segregation of immigrants in Japan, using South Africa's apartheid as an example, and faced widespread criticism as a consequence.[17] Last, Reiko Mori (1928–2014) and Yoshiko Shigekuni (1939–1985) were

---

13 https://en.wikipedia.org/wiki/Hanako_Muraoka

14 The cross *Pro Ecclesia et Pontifice* ('For Church and Pope') is a Holy See decoration now bestowed upon laypeople and clergy for remarkable service in the Catholic Church.

15 Even if my social and political beliefs differ from Sono's, it was necessary to include her in my work for the sake of objectivity.

16 https://www.japantimes.co.jp/community/2013/09/23/issues/matahara-turning-the-clock-back-on-womens-rights/#.UkhGq9KJN14

17 http://www.japantimes.co.jp/news/2015/02/12/national/author-sono-calls-racial-segregation-op-ed-piece/

two other women novelists whose writings were directly or indirectly motivated by their personal lives as women and their religion, Christianity.

Theology

In Japan, significant women Christian theologians emerged in the postwar era. Among them, many academics have concentrated on studying and teaching various topics within theology or been feminist theologians who speak out about issues concerning women within the church and in society. Japanese feminist theologians are widely represented in journals and books on Asian women theologians, including *In God's Image: Journal of Asian Women's Resource Center for Culture and Theology.* Tomoko Yamashita, Eun Ja Lee, Kazumi Usui, Satoko Yamaguchi, Yuko Yuasa, Megumi Yoshida, Nobuko Uesawa, and Yuri Horie are only a few of Japan's numerous feminist theologians to be mentioned here.

Satoko Yamaguchi (1945–) is by far the best-known feminist theologian, one who works both in Japan and internationally. Yamaguchi is primarily interested in critical feminist and postcolonial philosophy when it comes to religion. She was awarded the Bible & Archeology prize for her dissertation at the Episcopal Divinity School in Cambridge, Massachusetts, and taught at the New York Theological Seminary and the Newark School of Theology. Currently a professor at Japan Biblical Theological Seminary (Protestant), Central Theological College (Episcopal), Keisen Women's University (Protestant), and Sacred Heart University in Tokyo (Catholic), she is also the co-director of Japan's Center for Feminist Theology and Ministry. Her work *Mary and Martha: Women in the World of Jesus* won the Catholic Press

Association's 2003 Book Award in the United States and Canada. Hisako Kinukawa is a prominent theologian who co-directs the Center for Feminist Theology and Ministry with Yamaguchi. Her best-known work is *Women and Jesus in Mark: A Japanese Feminist Perspective (1994)*.

Haruko Nawata Ward is another well-known Japanese theologian, whose research interests include the Reformation, Jesuits, cross-cultural and religious interaction, women and religious vocation, the history of biblical interpretation, Christianity in Asia, and questions of justice in the history of the Catholic Church. She is the well-known author of *Women Religious Leaders in Japan's Christian Century, 1549–1650,* used as a secondary source in Chapter 1.

In 1988, Rita Nakashima Brock (1951-) became the first Asian American woman to earn a doctorate in theology. Born in 1950 in Fukuoka, Japan, she has been a pioneering voice in various fields of theological and civic discourse, ranging from feminist theology to the *Truth Commission on Wartime Conscience* (2010). Taking the call of love to justice seriously, Nakashima Brock's theology is deeply relational while also addressing systemic oppression and abuse. A feminist academic, Protestant theologian, activist, and leader of a nonprofit organization in the United States, she is also the senior vice president for Moral Injury Programs at Volunteers of America in Alexandria, Virginia, and a Christian Church-commissioned minister (i.e., Disciples of Christ). *Saving Paradise: How Christianity Traded the Love of this World to Crucifixion and Empire* is one of her most famous theological works, one that *Publishers Weekly* ranked among the best books on religion in 2008.

Eiko Takamizawa (1955 -), is another well-known theologian, a retired professor of intercultural studies at Torch Trinity University in South Korea. She was the first Japanese woman missiologist to join the University's faculty and serves as president of the Asian Society of Missiology. Takamizawa is the founder and the representative for the supporters' association of *Mongol Kids' Home: Support Manhole Children*. She launched this project in 2018 to care for abandoned and ignored Mongolian children by providing a safe home-like environment so that each child will maximize the gifts of life and talents for the community, society, and the world!

Women in the Church

Traditionally and historically, women have carried out many day-to-day activities and social roles within the church. Although women represent most churchgoers and have long been the numerical majority in the pews as well, they have nevertheless

> remained in the minority in decision-making positions, such as heads of committees and boards, in the church. Moreover, while women are the majority in the active workforce, it is not unusual that men are nominated as representatives of many groups and movements, despite their poor participation. This tendency results in women's invisibility even in today's church annals, which record only representative names in annual church reports. (Yamaguchi 2003, 317)

Yamaguchi (2003) has suggested that Christian women feel treated as second-class citizens in their faith communities, both ethnically and sexually, and argues that when it comes to women in religious traditions, since 1975, the International Women's Year, women have been relatively slow to support sexual equality. However, they have been active in various movements, primarily about war, peace, nuclear proliferation, environment, human rights, and equality. The Christian women themselves have expressed belief in the divine biblical notion of gender roles and division, which Yamaguchi (2003) believes has resulted from European theology oriented toward white men. By the end of the 20th century, an increasing number of women began to question that understanding in Christian and other spiritual traditions.

Hisako Kinukawa (2003) has contended that the cause of the inequality is rooted in the way that the Bible is translated and interpreted in Japanese. She had added that many original texts are translated into Japanese in ways that affirm the traditional patriarchal view of women and men in Japan. Scriptures related to women have thus been neglected in churches, where few people know that such Biblical texts exist. Even texts advocating equality between men and women are read exclusively for men's benefit (Kinukawa 2003, 1). In the book *Women Moving Mountains*, Kinukawa has shared her experience: "I was dissatisfied with the middle-class Western male interpretation that for so long had been forced on us as the 'unbiased objective and therefore correct' interpretation of the Bible" (Chun, Isshiki, Kinukawa and Yamaguchi, 2000, 60). Kinukawa was a member of the *mu-kyokai* ('non-church') movement, founded by Kanzo Uchimura (1861–1930), which was not initially intended to be an organized church. Instead, its emphasis was on the indigenization of

Christianity without Western doctrinal control, although it evolved into an organized movement with organized meetings over time. Even though the non-church movement was considered to be a new, open movement within Christianity, its founder, Uchimura, did not support women in church and ministry leadership. Uchimura adhered to Japanese patriarchal traditions as well as a literal interpretation of the Bible. According to Kinukawa:

> Mu-kyokai was no exception when it comes to a history of discrimination against women. The biblical passages such as "Christ is the head of every man, and the husband is the head of his wife, and God is the head of Christ" and "Let a woman learn in silence with full submission. I permit no woman to teach or to have authority over a man; she is to keep silent" has a strong impact on the teachings regarding how women were to behave in and outside the movement. At the gathering I regularly attended, the seats for men and those for women were clearly separated. While men gathered to make decisions, women worked in the kitchen. The gender role system was accepted and applied to the communal life of the movement without question. (Chun, Isshiki, Kinukawa and Yamaguchi, 2000, 59)

Tomoko Yamashita (2009) has acknowledged that though Protestant churches have accepted women as pastors, that trend has steadily shifted such that it is now difficult for women to acquire leadership roles in Japan. Even if women have all the necessary qualifications, they find it challenging to become senior pastors (Yamashita 2009, 5). Despite internal opposition, Yamashita became the first woman senior pastor of Aizuwakamatsu Church, of the United Church of Christ, which was founded in 1886 by Joseph (Jo) H. Neesima (1843–1890) in response to his wife Yae Neesima's (1845–1932) desire to establish a church in Aizu (Yamashita 2009, 3).

Satoru Kanemoto, who served as president of the Asia-Pacific Church of God Conference in 2019, suggests that although some women pastors are fairly influential in Japan, their social position often reflects a supportive instead of a leading role. For instance, a large Japanese seminary employs five professors but has never appointed a woman professor, despite efforts to overcome numerous dividing walls. As a result, certain women preachers have to bear the weight of breaking free from the present theological paradigm.[18]

Yoshiko Isshiki became a pastor at quite a late stage in her life. While her children were entering university, she joined Tokyo Union Theological Seminary, and after passing the exams, she was ordained as a pastor in her church, where she served before as a lay leader and elder. In time, she became pastor of Kyodo Midorigaoka Church in the 1980s.

The United Church of Christ Japan (UCCJ), Japan's largest Protestant church, appointed the country's first woman pastor in 1930. According to Chun, Isshiki, Kinukawa, and Yamaguchi (2000, 29), the UCCJ had ordained more than 240 women as pastors by 2000, which accounted for nearly

---

18 https://www.jesusisthesubject.org/japan-celebrates-increasing-number-of-women-in-ministry/

one-fifth of the total number of pastors in the church. The United Church of Japan ordained its first woman pastor in 1952. Years later, unlike in the Roman Catholic Church, Ikuko Williams was ordained as Japan's first woman priest by the Anglican Church of Japan in 2007.

Despite an increasing number of women pastors, priests, and ministers in Japan, most churches are pastored by men. On top of that, most critical decisions are made by men, even though women are the majority. Although church culture in Japan continues to be patriarchal, the march toward equality continues. The following chapter explores Japanese feminist theology and discusses the opinions of some prominent feminist theologians from Japan.

Japanese
WOMEN
& CHRISTIANITY

WOMEN, CULTURE,

& Feminist Theology in Japan

Chapter Five

WOMEN, CULTURE,
& Feminist Theology in Japan

The introductory chapter states that Japan's mythological birth began with a woman, the sun goddess, with the implication that women's elevated role is limited to myths and stories. Indeed, Japanese culture has been dominated by Confucian ideals that position men superior to women, Buddhist ideas that emphasize women's pollution, and Shinto ones that forbid women from entering certain sacred places. Although Christianity has improved women's status, it nevertheless adheres to patriarchal ecclesiastical and theological practices. Yamaguchi (2003, 319) indicates that

> outside of the church, there was a growing number of women who felt a spiritual thirst but were disappointed by the church. They would say, "We were attracted to the teaching in Christianity that there is no male and female before God. But when we participated in church services and activities, we found that the basic church structure is no different than that of society: men speak while women listen, and men make decisions in meeting rooms while women stand in the kitchen. Surely, church-going women are doubly pushed, not only by Japanese culture/society but also by the church, to accept the dualistic gender concept as natural or divinely given. Few ministers are sensitized to these "women's

concerns. The church has not been responding to the spiritual thirst of these women either.

In response to those trends, this chapter offers a brief overview of how women are portrayed in Japanese culture, particularly as reflected in the Japanese language, before proceeding to a short discussion of contemporary Japanese feminism and concluding with a perspective on feminist theology in Japan. To be sure, viewpoints on women's roles in Japanese culture vary. One is from a patriarchal perspective, which requires women to be corporate warriors by being so-called "professional housewives" in their early married lives while being accessible for work in their later married years. Especially in the 1980s, when the Japanese economy flourished, the notion of women serving their hardworking husbands as housewives was the norm, despite feminist views to the contrary. Such concepts were linked to Japanism, the idea of a corporate, united Japan as a family, with a strong focus on Japan's traditional values, which may be traced back to Buddhism and Confucianism.

Before the idea of professional housewives, there existed the *ryōsai-kenbo* ('good wife and wise mother'), a construct of nation-state Japan from the beginning of Japan's modernization, industrialization, and militarism in 1868 to the end of World War II. The concept of the professional housewife subsequently supplanted the good wife and wise mother. Some have argued that the notion of a good wife and wise mother is more connected to European conceptions of women in the 19th century and the early Meiji period than to Confucian and Buddhist concepts in the Tokugawa period. On that point, Ochiai and Johshita (2014, 155) have written:

However, in the 1980s, research questioned this view. Koyama Shizuko discovered that the phrase 'ryōsai-kenbo' was not to be found anywhere in records from the time of the Tokugawa Shogunate. Its first appearance was at the end of the nineteenth century and actually followed the influence of European ideas of women in the early Meiji period.

Feminism, however, challenges the patriarchy and views such ideas as a form of women's oppression. Yoshiko Kanai (1996, 17) has described women's oppression based on ancient Japanese traditions and culture as "cultural deconstructive feminism." According to Kanai, based on Foucault's theory of power, women's oppression in Japan can be found in the structures of invisible power functions, which are organized and anchored in language and discourse, thereby entrenching women's subjectivity within a linguistic order centered around men. As a result, women internalize oppression and join subordinate relationships involuntarily (Kanai 1996, 17). Such internalization of oppression may also be relevant to discuss about the Christian patriarchy, as evidenced by scriptural interpretations and as examined in this chapter.

As a case in point, Hisako Kinukawa (2003, 33) has written about the so-called "labeling" of women by adherents of patriarchal authority:

> The powers-that-be need that kind of social structure for keeping their status quo as well as their integrity. The woman's hemorrhage threatens the community's integrity and its holiness, just as women's bleeding and childbirth have threatened the holiness and integrity of the male-dominant structure of our

society. What she earnestly seeks is the recovery of her "wholeness and holiness" so that she may be accepted as a person within the circle of society. In a patriarchal society where hierarchical class strata are strictly maintained, the boundary between the pure and the impure becomes very important. To make it hard to cross barriers, socially banned persons are given another label of being contagious and are abhorred. It is necessary for authority to keep her invisible. In order for her to come out of the closed world, the boundary between her and the rest of society must be broken down.

Women in the Japanese Language

Language is one of the most powerful labeling factors in any society. As Saul Alinsky correctly observed, "He who controls the language controls the people" and, in turn, culture and society.[1] The way women are branded in a specific language reveals a great deal about their social status in culture and society. Kittredge Cherry and Naoko Takemaru have each written on the topic of language and women. Whereas Cherry's work discusses what Japanese words reveal about women in Japan, especially in *Womansword* (2002), Takemaru's book *Women in the Language and Society of Japan* (2010) examines the linguistic origins of gender prejudice.

The Japanese language consists of three writing systems: *hiragana, katakana,* and *kanji.* Whereas katakana is a phonetic alphabet used to transcribe foreign words, in

---

1   https://moellerlit.weebly.com/uploads/1/0/2/4/10248653/1984_--_
    vree_article_on_language.pdf

particular, *hiragana* is a phonetic alphabet that women were allowed to write and communicate in the 7th century CE, when women were not permitted to use the kanji writing system imported from China. Kanji, meanwhile, is a symbolic writing system that may be likened to the emojis used in digital communication today. Although kanji characters may be used to write anything in Japanese, when paired with other kanji characters, certain ones can assume a different meaning.

According to Cherry, the kanji character 女 *(onna)*, for example, used in Japanese to denote 'woman' or 'female,' already reveals much about how women have been regarded in Japanese linguistic culture. In particular, combining the character with others creates words that reveal a lot about how women were portrayed in Japan's ancient patriarchal society. The verb meaning 'to be jealous,' for instance, is a mix of the characters for 'woman 女' and 'illness 疾' (Cherry 2002, 31) 嫉, thereby suggesting that jealousy is essentially an illness experienced by women. The word for 'tease' *(naburu* 嬲*)* combines the kanji characters for women 女 and two kanji characters for men 男; as a result, the kanji character for 'to tease' is sometimes used in conjunction with the character for 'murder' to mean 'death through torment' *(naburi-goroshi).* Moreover, the kanji character for 'woman 女,' when repeated three times, means 'noisy' or 'evil 姦' *(kashimashii;* Cherry 2002, 31). Such combinations of kanji characters with the single character for 'woman' reveal deeply ingrained conventional cultural biases.

Linguistic expressions about women in Japan are also quite telling. For example, *hako-iri musume* literally means 'daughters in a box' (Cherry 2002, 41), meaning that precious dolls, scrolls, and other items should be stored in wooden boxes to protect them from the evils of the world (Cherry 2002, 41). Even though the phrase is widely accepted in society, it demonstrates what Kinukawa (2003) is quoted as writing earlier in the chapter about "the need for the dominant power to keep women invisible." Although the linguistic confinement of women in a box is ostensibly for her benefit, in reality it benefits the patriarchal ruling class.

Among other examples, the phrase *onna datera ni* ('unlike a woman' or 'unsuitable for a woman') is used to condemn a woman's conduct that violates society's code or standards for femininity (Takemaru 2010, 107). The saying *dakara onna wa dameda* ('that's why women are no good') has an exceptionally negative meaning for women (Takemaru 2010, 107); the saying is often used when men are annoyed with their wives, sisters, girlfriends, or colleagues. In Japanese, they also call a cowardly or indecisive man *onna no kusatta yōna*, which literally means 'like a rotten woman.' Even though men use the phrase to criticize other men, the more significant underlying insult is the implication that they are women *(onna)*. Another term is *shokuba no hana* ('office flowers'), used for young office workers who are women to characterize them with "short-lived blossoming" (Cherry 2002, 105). Such young women are thus compared to ornaments and decorations intended to uplift the spirit of men in the office. They do not do heavy work but serve tea, make copies, and/or answer phones (Cherry 2002, 105).

As shown by the above examples, biases against women are intertwined within both written linguistic codes, concealed in kanji symbols, and spoken words and phrases. However, such preconceptions and biases are not exclusive to Japan but confronted by all women around the world.

Feminism in Contemporary Japan

In Japanese, the word *feminisuto* ('feminist'), derived from *feminizumu* ('feminism'), has two definitions: a courteous man who treats women with respect or a person who fights for emancipation and equality rights for women. Both definitions are widely found in Japanese dictionaries (Takemaru 2010, 79). Takemaru has argued that many people believe that feminism in contemporary Japan was inspired by and imitated from American women's liberation movements, particularly in the 1970s.[2]

The second wave of feminism in Japan, cresting in the 1990s, is seen to be unique to Japan and a few other Asian countries. According to Takemaru (2010, 79), "A number of comparative studies of Western and Japanese feminist models have also been conducted, the majority of which conclude that Western feminist models are not applicable to Japanese counterparts." Women's liberation via Japanese feminism in the 1990s was primarily concerned with redefining women's identity outside the conventional Japanese cultural structures supporting norms that confine women to the roles of professional housewives and excellent moms.

---

2 Japan's initial exposure to American feminism in the late 1960s and 1970s focused on mass media events, women protests, and nudity protests. Japanese media, in being dominated by men, thus portrayed the feminists depicted as being eccentric and constantly criticized how the so-called "women's liberation movement in Japan" copied American feminism (Takemaru, 80).

Feminist Theology in Japanese Context

In Japan, feminism seems to have been primarily concerned with breaking away from cultural norms imposed on women. Some of those norms have already been covered in earlier chapters. When it comes to feminist theology in Japan, Takemaru's (2010) description is backed up by Hisako Kinukawa. According to Kinukawa (2003, 16), in Japan, "It seems that 'shame' and not 'honor' functions as the standard norms, a culture of 'shame/honor' in comparison with the culture of 'honor/shame.'" She has argued that "the negative expression 'avoiding disgraceful conduct' was engendered by Confucian teachings: 'pay due reverence to anyone above'" and that "in general, women have been trained to sacrifice themselves for men, not to lose face and to keep up appearances." In that sense, it may be plausible that women have been shouldered with the "shame of the society," which she compares with first-century Palestine (Kinukawa 2003, 17).

Kinukawa (2003, 20) has also discussed women's "subconscious enslavement" in believing that they must be obedient, keep silent, and be invisible behind their husbands. Such beliefs about women can also be found in the Bible, and traditional Christians in Japan continue to maintain them. Early missionaries, both during the Tokugawa period and eras up to the postwar period in Japan, held similar beliefs. However, feminist theologians such as Kinukawa have breathed new life into biblical readings about women. In her book *Woman and Jesus in Mark: A Japanese Feminist Perspective* (2003), she delves into the Book of Mark's encounters between women and Christ, each of which is viewed as liberating, empowering, and freeing women from the oppression of religion and tradition. From that perspective, she draws parallels between those experiences, Israel and cultural Palestine's religious environment at the time, and her background informed by the patriarchy in Japan. She particularly compares the story of the women with the issue of blood, who tried to touch Christ to be healed (Mark 5:24–34) with the story of outcasts in Japan who are labeled as unclean and thus segregated from society simply for being members of the outcast class.

Well-known outcasts in Japan include, for example, the *burakumin*. The term *burakumin* ('hamlet people') refers to Japan's traditional "unclean" caste, also known as *eta* ('filthy mass') and *hinin* ('nonhuman'). During the Tokugawa period, the *burakumin* were forced to live in separate villages and perform society's dirty work, including grave digging, butchery, executions, and other abhorrent jobs. Nearly 2% of Japanese people are *buraku*, and despite being racially identical to other Japanese people, they are frequently discriminated against. Trapped in a vicious cycle of prejudice and poverty, many of the *burakumin* are forced to fabricate sanitized family histories. Although the class was officially abolished in a parliamentary act in 1871, employers commonly check the background of applicants for buraku heritage.[3] Because of that dynamic, Kinukawa (2003, 20) has written that laws and constitutions "cannot transform human mentality or consciousness so easily." Thus, just as menstruating women sought a miracle by making contact with Christ, so the outcasts of Japan, who lived in segregated villages, touched churches. She cites an example from 1922 when the outcasts of Japan came with their declaration of

---

3 http://www.japanfortheuninvited.com/articles/burakumin.html

human rights based on the Christian faith even though they were not Christians (Kinukawa 2003, 40).

Satoko Yamaguchi, the abovementioned feminist theologian, in her award-winning book *Mary and Martha: Women in the World of Jesus* (2002) examines women's problems through the lens of the Gospel of John. By reimagining Martha's and Mary's roles in the narrative from a Japanese viewpoint, she encourages revisionism and a new historical imagination. From a liberationist viewpoint, her feminist theology addresses the oppression of women and other groups of people in the Bible by contextualizing them in their historical and cultural settings:

> Looking anew at Christian history from women's perspective involves re-visioning the history of human beings, their experiences of the god, and our present and the future. It is a collaborative venture that can not succeed without integrating insights gained from diverse experiences and a variety of fields. It also involves restoring a diachronic historical network of women that was distorted, made invisible, and cut off by male-centered patriarchal society, and at the same time constructing a synchronical geographical network of diverse women. (Chun, Isshiki, Kinukawa and Yamaguchi 2000, 121)

Chun, Isshiki, Kinukawa, and Yamaguchi (2000, 122) have suggested: "that historically, Christian theology has involved interpretations of events that took place in first-century Mediterranean culture through the eyes of the Western culture of later generations." That tradition warrants change, however, and academics, both men and women but particularly feminist theologians from non-Western backgrounds, should reexamine and reinterpret their historical, cultural, and social contexts in light of the Gospel. As Japanese theologians, those authors have examined the image of the transcendent and absolute God, for example, through the lens of Japanese history and its ritual religion, Shintoism, which has numerous gods who dwell and mingle with humans, lack dogmatic development, and have been conveniently used by political authorities for non-religious purposes. The authors, seeking spirituality and theology beyond patriarchy, thus argue that providing their critical viewpoint may help to reexamine Shinto deities and reevaluate dogma and rituals (Chun, Isshiki, Kinukawa and Yamaguchi 2000, 122).

In Japan, feminist theology is often approached from a liberationist viewpoint and addresses comfort women, particularly from Korea, as well as exclusion based on gender, gender orientation, ethnic minorities, and untouchables— that is, the so-called "unclean." Japan's feminist theologians also address issues of justice, peace, human rights, and antinuclear policy and, perhaps more critically, reexamine, reinterpret, and reimagine the presence and role of women in biblical tales, as well as in the often unvoiced, often purposely neglected, and underappreciated histories of women in Japan and beyond.

SUMMARY
& CLOSING REMARKS

SUMMARY
& CLOSING REMARKS

The account of Christian women in Japan represents only one account of the millions of Christian women around the world. Since the inception of the Christian church, women have played an essential part in disseminating the Gospel worldwide, such that Christianity is arguably a religion most truly held by women, who have performed critical duties in carrying the cross of Christ's love forward. Nevertheless, patriarchalism within Christian teachings has also arguably made women second-class citizens in the church. Such interpretations of Christian teachings have led clerics in the past and present to think that women should stay silent, for so says Paul and many other parts of the Bible (1 Corinthians 14:34–35).

This book indeed offers proof that women have been crucial in developing Christianity in Japan since its arrival in the country in the 16th century. Even when the religion was banned and Christians were persecuted, women continued to be essential in spreading Christian doctrine. Until the late 19th century, women such as Julia Naitō (1566–1627) and Gracia Tama Hosokawa (1563–1600) played vital roles in Christian life, including as translators, writers, teachers (e.g., catechists and apologists), debaters, lecturers, evangelists, charity workers, and social activists, even in an era when women in Japan and worldwide had few rights.

During the Tokugawa period, women died as martyrs: some alone and some with their infants in their arms. They never abandoned their belief in Christ nor their loyalty to the church. Even so, the stories of those women in Japan are marginalized and partly disregarded, and some were destroyed during the period of Christian persecution, thus leaving little for the world to read and learn from. Perhaps Western Christians would not have known about the work, suffering, and sacrifice of their sisters in Japan for the Gospel if Haruko Nawata Ward (2009) had not written her profound work *Women Religious Leaders in Japan's Christian Century, 1549–1650.*

When Japan began modernizing in 1868 with the Meiji Restoration, Christian women gradually became involved in evangelism, social work, and advocacy for women's human rights and right to education. During that time, prominent missionaries, particularly women, inspired Christian women in Japan and provided them with the foundations for education, human rights, and activism, thereby nurturing native Christian women in Japan able to carry forth the Gospel and impact Japanese society in the years to come. A prime example is Umeko Tsuda (1864-1929), who believed that all women in Japan should have equal access to higher education and that only education could help improve women's status in the country. Putting those ideas in practice, she established an institute for women to study English that after World War II became Tsuda University, one of the most prestigious women's colleges in Japan. In 1905, Tsuda also became the first president of the Japanese branch of the World Young Women's Christian Association.

Other examples were Hatsune Hasegawa (1890–1979) and Tamaki Kawado Uemura, who ranked among the first women pastors in Japan at the time. Beyond that, Ginko Ogino (1851–1913) was the first woman doctor in Japan to receive a degree in Western medicine. Ogino married Yukiyoshi Shikata, a Protestant minister, in 1890, and in 1894, she relocated with him to Hokkaido where they operated a medical practice. In 1908, following her husband's death, she returned to Tokyo and began running a hospital. She was also a member of the Woman's Christian Temperance Union.

After World War II, inspired by their faith, Christian women in Japan contributed to many art forms, including literature, cinema, manga, and music. Among them, Machiko Hasegawa (1920–1992) was one of Japan's first woman manga artists, and Kelly Kozumi Shinozawa, is a contemporary Christian manga artist best known for her works *The Manga Messiah* and *The Manga Bible Series*, translated into 21 languages worldwide, and who received the Albums Primes Manga Grand Award in 2010. Other renowned women theologians can be found in Japan, including Satoko Yamaguchi, a well-known feminist theologian who works in Japan and around the world; Haruko Nawata Ward, a historian known for her *Women Religious Leaders in Japan's Christian Century, 1549–1650;* and Rita Nakashima Brock, who in 1988 became the first Asian-American woman to receive a doctorate in theology.

Ultimately, not only have Japan's renowned Christian women influenced Japan with the Gospel but also all of the nameless mothers, sisters, spouses, partners, and friends who have quietly continued to serve the church and society. Although no one knows their names, and no one has ever recorded their tales, they are unsung heroines of God's kingdom.

In closing, I do not regard myself as a great scholar, nor did I set out to produce a comprehensive academic book on women in Japan and Christianity that would capture all of their contributions to the church and society. My sole purpose in this work is to share the knowledge contained herein with the rest of the world. Nevertheless, I sincerely hope that my contribution will help missionaries, churches, and evangelists working in or among the Japanese people to comprehend the Japanese context better and, as a result, more effectively share the Gospel with Japanese people.

I also hope that this book will inspire and empower women worldwide, especially in Japan, to pursue equality and justice for women. I especially want to encourage women who read this book by saying that there are always brothers who will stand by their side and raise with them the flag of equality and justice, and I am humbly one of them.

In Solidarity!

BIBLIOGRAPHY

BIBLIOGRAPHY

Adolphson, M., Kamens, E. and Matsumoto, S. (2007). *Heian Japan, Centers asnd Peripheries.* Honolulu: University of Hawai'i Press.

Ambros, B. R. (2015). *Women in Japanese Religions.* New York: New York University Press.

Bernard, M. (1926). *Japan's Martyr Church.* Exeter: Catholic Records Press.

Bestor, T. C. (1991) "Japanese Social Organization" in *Recreating Japanese Women, 1600–1945.* Bernstein, Gail Lee (ed.). Berkeley: University of California Press.

Boxer, C. R. (1993). *The Christian Century in Japan 1549–1650.* Manchester, UK: Carcanet Press Limited.

Cherry, K. (2002). *Womansword: What Japanese Words Say About Women.* Tokyo: Kodansha International.

Chun, K.-R., Isshiki, Y., Kinukawa, H. and Yamaguchi, S. (2000) *Women Moving Mountains.* Kuala Lumpur: AWRC.

Crawcour, S. (1974). "The Tokugawa Period and Japan's Preparation for Modern Economic Growth" *Journal of Japanese Studies* 1 (1): 113–124.

Dore, R.P. (1965). *Education in Tokugawa Japan*. London: Routledge & Kegan Paul.

Drummond, R. H. (1971). *A History of Christianity in Japan*. Grand Rapids, MI: Wm. B. Eerdmans.

Faison, E. (2017). "Women's Rights as Proletarian Rights: Yamakawa Kikue, Suffrage, and the 'Dawn of Liberation'" in *Rethinking Japanese Feminism*, Bullock, Julia C., Kano, Ayako and Welker, James (eds.). Honolulu: University of Hawai'i Press.

Fujiwara-Fanselow, K. and Kameda, A. (1995). *Japanese Women: New Feminist Perspectives on the Past, Present and Future*. New York: Feminist Press.

Hagemann, E. 1942. "The Persecution of the Christians in Japan in the Middle of the Seventeenth Century" in *Pacific Historical Review*, 11(2), pp. 151–160.

Hall, J. W. (1991). *Japan: Prehistory to Modern Times*. Frankfurt am Main: S. Fischer Verlag.

Hirata, K. and Warschauer, M. (2014). *Japan: The Paradox of Harmony*. New Haven: Yale University Press.

Holloway, S. D. (2010). *Women and Family in Contemporary Japan*. New York: Cambridge University Press.

Howe, S. W. (1995). "The Role of Women in the Introduction of Western Music in Japan" *Music Education*, 16(2): 81–97.

Kanai, Y. (1996). "The Women's Movement: Issues for Japanese Feminism" in *Voices from the Japanese Women's Movement*, AMPO: Japan Asia Quarterly Review (ed.). New York: M.E. Sharpe.

Kawai, M. and Kubushiro, O. (1934). *Japanese Women Speak: A Message from the Christian Women of Japan to the Christian Women of America*. Brattleboro: Vermont Printing Company.

Kinukawa, H. (2003). *Women and Jesus in Mark: A Japanese Feminist Perspective*. Eugene: Wipf and Stock Publishers.

Kohiyama, R. (1992). *Amerika fujin senkyōshi: Rainichi no haikei to sono eikyō* アメリカ婦人宣教 師 来日の背景と その影響. Tokyo: Tōkyō Daigaku Shuppankai.

Kohls, G G. "The Bombing of Nagasaki August 9, 1945: The Untold Story." https://medicolegal.tripod.com/ kohlsnagasaki-untold-story.htm

Lande, A. (1989). *Meiji Protestantism in History and Historiography*. Frankfurt-am-Main: Verlag Peter Lang GmbH.

Lebra, J. C. (1991). "Women in All-Male Industry" in *Recreating Japanese Women, 1600–1945*. Bernstein, Gail Lee (ed.). Berkeley: University of California Press.

Lee, S. (2015). *Understanding Japan Through the Eyes of Christian Faith* (5th ed.). Amsterdam: Foundation University Press.

Lublin, E. D. (2010). *Reforming Japan: The Woman's Christian Temperance Union in the Meiji Period*. Vancouver: University of British Colombia Press.

Marnas, F. (1896). *La religion de Jésus ressuscitée au Japon dans las seconde moitié du XIX siècle, Vol. 1*. Paris: Delhomme et Briguet.

Maxson, H. (2017). "From 'Motherhood in the Interest of the State' to Motherhood in the Interest of Mothers Rethinking the First Mothers' Congress" in *Rethinking Japanese Feminism,* Bullock, Julia C., Kano, A. and Welker, J. Honolulu: University of Hawai'i Press.

Meyvis, L. and Vande W. W. (1989). *Japan: Het Onvoltooide Experiment* (Japan: The Unfinished Experiment). Tielt: Drukkerij- Uitgeverij Lanno.

Molony, B. (1993). "The Japanese Debate Over Motherhood Protection, 1015–1950" in *Japanese Women Working,* Hunter, Janet (ed.). London: Routledge.

Muto, I. (1997). "The Birth of the Women's Liberation Movement in the 1970s" in *The Other Japan,* Moore, Joe (ed.). Armonk: M.E. Sharpe.

Ochiai, E. and Johshita, K. (2014). "Prime Ministers' Discourse in Japan's Reforms Since the 1980s: Traditionalization of Modernity Instead of Confucianism" in *Gender and Welfare States in East Asia Confucianism or Gender Equality?* Sung, Sirin and Pascall, Gillian (eds.). New York: Palgrave Macmillan.

Ogawa, M. (2004). "Rescue Work for Japanese Women: The Birth and Development of the Jiaikan Rescue Home and the Missionaries of the Woman's Christian Temperance Union, Japan, 1886–1921" in *U.S.–Japan Women's Journal,* 26: 98–133.

Ogasawara, Y. (2019). "Working Women's Husbands as Helpers of Partners" in *Beyond the Gender Gap in Japan,* Steel, Gill (ed.). Ann Arbor: University of Michigan Press.

Paramore, K. (2009). *Ideology and Christianity in Japan*. Oxford: Routledge.

Patessio, M. (2011). "Foreign Female Missionaries and Their Japanese Female Charges" in *Women in Public Life in Early Meiji Japan*. Ann Arbor: University of Michigan Press.

Prichard, M. N. and Prichard, N. Y. (1957). *Ten Against the Storm*. New York: Friendship Press.

Reischauer, E. O. and Craig, A. M. (1989). *Japan: Tradition & Transformation*. St. Leonards: Allen & Unwin Pty LTD.

Robertson, J. (1992). "Doing and Undoing 'Female' and 'Male' in Japan: The Takarazuka Revue" in *Japanese Social Organization*, Lebra, Takie Sugiyama (ed.). Honolulu: University of Hawai'i Press.

Rodd, L. R. (1991). "Yosano Akiko and the Taishō Debate Over the 'New Woman'" in *Recreating Japanese Women*, 1600–1945. Bernstein, Gail Lee (ed.). Berkeley: University of California Press.

Rose, B. (1992). *Tsuda Umeko and Women's Education in Japan*, New Haven: Yale University Press.

Sander, A. (2016). *Gracia Hosokaw: Ihr Leben und ihre Bedeutung als Frau und als Christin*. Munich: Grin Verlag.

Seat, K. (2003). "Mission Schools and Education for Women" in *Handbook of Christianity in Japan*. Mark R. Mullins (ed.). Leiden: Brill.

Shibahara, T. (2010). "Through Americanized Japanese Woman's Eyes: Tsuda Umeko and the Women's Movement in Japan in the 1910s" in *Journal of Asia Pacific Studies*, 1(2): 225–234.

Sievers, S. L. (1983). *Flowers in Salt: The Beginning of Feminist Consciousness in Modern Japan*. Stanford: Stanford University Press.

Silva, M. A. (2010). "Women in Ancient Japan: From Matriarchal Antiquity to Acquiescent Confinement." *Inquiries Journal* 2(9):1-1. http://www.inquiriesjournal. com/articles/286/women-in-ancient-japan-from-matriarchal-antiquity-to-acquiescent-confinement

Takemaru, N. (2010). *Women in the Language and Society of Japan: The Linguistic Roots of Bias*. Jefferson: McFarland & Company.

Walthall, A. (1991). "Life Cycle of Farm Woman in Tokugawa Japan" in *Recreating Japanese Women, 1600–1945*. Bernstein, Gail Lee (ed.). Berkeley: University of California Press.

Ward, H. N. (2012). "Women and Kirishitanban Literature: Translation, Gender, and Theology in *Early Modern Japan*" in Early Modern Women, 7:271–281.

Ward, H. N. (2009). *Women Religious Leaders in Japan's Christian Century, 1549-1650*. Women and Gender in the Early Modern World. Farnham etc.: Ashgate.

Watanabe, M. (1991). "Women's Issues" in *Christianity in Japan 1971–90*, Yoshinobu, Kumazawa and Swain, David L. (eds.), Tokyo: Kyo Bun Kwan.

Worsley, P. (1964). *The Third World*. London: Weidenfeld and Nicolson.

Yamaguchi, S. (2003). "Christianity and Women in Japan" in *Japanese Journal of Religious Studies* 30/3–4: 315–338, Nagoya: Nanzan Institute for Religion and Culture.

Yamaguchi, S. (2006). *Mary and Martha: Women in the World of Jesus*. Eugene: Wipf and Stock Publishers.

Yamashita, T. (2009). "Dressing Like Myself: My Experience as a Female Pastor: Globally Diverse Voices of Women Doing Feminist Theology in Japan," in *In God's Image: Journal of Asian Women's Resource Centre for Culture and Theology*. 28(4).

ACKNOWLEDGEMENTS

My thanks go to everyone who has helped me make this book a reality, particularly Tim Gilman, Rev. Masahiro Ogawa, Rev. Dr. Nelson Jennings, Simon Pleasants, and many more who have supported me in the process of writing this book.

Many thanks also to the Spaan Foundation in the Netherlands for their support.

ABOUT THE AUTHOR

Samuel Lee is president of Foundation Academy of Amsterdam, an Academy for Liberal Arts and Humanities. Lee holds a Ph.D. in Theology from Vrije Universiteit Amsterdam, where he currently leads the Center for Theology of Migration. His Ph.D. is about Christianity in Japan.

Lee has a master's degree with a doctoral exam in Sociology of Non-Western Societies (with an emphasis on Japan) from Leiden University in the Netherlands. Samuel Lee is the author of *The Japanese and Christianity: Why is Christianity Not Widely Believed in Japan?* (2014).